Canada's favourite  r

Cestnick

Winning the
Education
Savings
Game

RESPs AND
OTHER STRATEGIES
FOR CANADIANS

PRENTICE HALL CANADA

Canadian Cataloguing in Publication Data
Cestnick, Timothy J., 1966–
     Winning the education savings game: RESPs and other strategies for
     Canadians

Annual.
[1999]-
ISSN 1490-8484
ISBN 0-13-022048-5 (1999 issue)

1. Education savings accounts – Canada 2. Finance, Personal – Canada. 3.
College costs – Canada. I. Title

HG179.C472   332.024'02   C99-901061-1

Prentice-Hall, Inc., Upper Saddle River, New Jersey
Prentice-Hall International (UK) Limited, London
Prentice-Hall of Australia, Pty. Limited, Sydney
Prentice-Hall Hispanoamericana, S.A., Mexico City
Prentice-Hall of India Private Limited, New Delhi
Prentice-Hall of Japan, Inc., Tokyo
Simon & Schuster Southeast Asia Private Limited, Singapore
Editora Prentice-Hall do Brasil, Ltda., Rio de Janeiro

ISBN 0-13-022048-5 (1999 issue)

Editorial Director, Trade Group: Andrea Crozier
Acquisitions Editor: Paul Woods
Copy Editor: Patricia Tolmie
Production Editor: Jodi Lewchuk
Art Direction: Mary Opper
Cover and Interior Design: Gary Beelik
Cover Image: Penny Gentieu/Tony Stone Images
Author and Family Photo: Kirk McGregor
Production Coordinator: Barbara Ollerenshaw
Page Layout: Art Plus

1 2 3 4 5   WC   03 02 01 00 99
Printed and bound in Canada

This publication contains the opinions and ideas of its author and is designed
to provide useful advice in regard to the subject matter covered. The author
and publisher are not engaged in rendering legal, accounting, or other professional services in this publication. This publication is not intended to provide
a basis for action in particular circumstances without consideration by a competent professional. The author and publisher expressly disclaim any responsibility for any liability. loss, or risk, personal or otherwise, which is incurred
as a consequence, directly or indirectly, of the use and application of any of
the contents of this book.

Visit the Prentice Hall Canada web site! Send us your comments, browse our
catalogues, and more at **www.phcanada.com**.

Dedication

To my son, Winston, and our second child on the way. And to my nieces and nephews: Lindsay, Logan, Jamie Ann, Alexi, Tori, Zuri, Lincoln, Chloe, Virginia, Sami, and another to arrive soon.

Acknowledgments

Writing a book of any length is an ambitious task for any one person. Fortunately, I've had the help of competent staff, family, and associates, making my job much easier. I'd like to thank Skye Fulton and her husband, Randy, for their hours of research. Without their hard work, this book would be half the size. Thanks also to Laura Giacomelli at my firm for her invaluable help with many of the important little details in getting this book ready. For their patience in waiting for me to finish this project, I'd like to thank my editor, Pat Tolmie, and the staff at Prentice Hall, particularly Paul Woods. The designers have done a terrific job—and so I thank them. My extended family deserves thanks for allowing me to use their names in this book (they could have said "No way"). Most importantly, a special thanks to my wife, Carolyn, who has demonstrated much patience and support despite the many hours I spent locked away writing this book.

Table of Contents

Education Planning Tip Sheet

This Education Planning Tip Sheet provides a summary of all the tips that I discuss in this book. It can be an invaluable tool that will help you to identify those tips that are of interest and most relevant to you and your family. It's not difficult to use. Start by reading a chapter, then come back here to review the tips for that chapter. For each tip, simply answer the question: Should I make note of this? Once you're done, revisit the *Yes* and *Not Sure* answers. These will form a list for further action. What kind of action? It depends on the tip. Some tips may require a talk with your spouse or kids. Some might call for a meeting with a financial adviser, a visit to your bank, a note in an "Education" file folder you've created, or a simple "post-it" note on your fridge.

This book has been designed to spur you to action in the area of planning for the education of that special child in your life. And this Education Planning Tip Sheet provides a foundation for the action you're going to take.

Tim's Tips	Strategy	Should I Make Note of This?		
		Yes	**No**	**Not Sure**
Chapter 2.	Mathematics 101: Calculating the Cost of Education			
1.	Avoid unpleasant surprises when it comes time to cut the first tuition cheque.	O	O	O
2.	Understand the trend of education costs over the last decade.	O	O	O
3.	Watch for signs that education costs will continue to soar.	O	O	O
4.	Compare our tuition fees to those in other countries to understand where we are globally.	O	O	O
5.	Don't distinguish between college and university costs when planning for the future.	O	O	O

Tim's Tips	Strategy	Should I Make Note of This?		
		Yes	**No**	**Not Sure**
6.	Consider when, where, and how your child will attend school when calculating the cost of your child's education.	○	○	○
7.	Understand that a higher percentage of jobs each year will require a post-secondary education.	○	○	○
8.	Understand that unemployment rates for those with a postsecondary education are much lower than for those without.	○	○	○
9.	Check out the expected rate of return from a postsecondary education. It can be attractive.	○	○	○
Chapter 3.	Economics 101: Paying for an Education			
10.	Look at a variety of ways to pay for your child's education.	○	○	○
11.	Start thinking about free money well ahead of time, not at the last minute.	○	○	○
12.	Know where to look for free money.	○	○	○
13.	Contact the federal and provincial governments for more information about free money available from them.	○	○	○
14.	Don't forget to set aside funds to cover the tax bill on your free money.	○	○	○
15.	Shake the trend that has students borrowing more than ever while making repayments at a slower pace.	○	○	○
16.	Look first to the Canada Student Loans Program when borrowing money.	○	○	○
17.	Look to your bank for a loan if your child doesn't qualify for the CSLP.	○	○	○
18.	Be sure to claim tax and other relief for interest paid on student loans.	○	○	○

Tim's Tips	Strategy	Should I Make Note of This?		
		Yes	No	Not Sure
19.	Don't declare bankruptcy to avoid student debt—better options are available.	○	○	○
20.	Use your lifestyle assets for education only as a last resort.	○	○	○
21.	Avoid dipping into your retirement assets at all costs.	○	○	○
22.	Plan to use some of your other cash resources for your child's education.	○	○	○
23.	Encourage your child to use employment as a means of raising money and gaining valuable experience.	○	○	○
24.	Encourage your child to look for jobs on campus.	○	○	○
25.	Keep work time to a maximum of 15 hours a week, since education is the number one priority	○	○	○
26.	Start saving for your child's education as soon as possible, and save regularly.	○	○	○
27.	Focus on equity investments and foreign content to improve returns over the long term.	○	○	○
28.	Stick to your investment strategy regardless of the box in which you hold your investments.	○	○	○
Chapter 4.	Woodworking 101: Building an Education Plan			
29.	Calculate the cost of your child's education as step 1 in building an education plan.	○	○	○
30.	Clarify your child's goals as step 2 in building an education plan.	○	○	○
31.	Compare and evaluate schools to determine which one is best as step 3 in building an education plan.	○	○	○

Tim's Tips	Strategy	Should I Make Note of This?		
		Yes	No	Not Sure
32.	Choose your child's sources of funding as step 4 in building an education plan.	○	○	○
33.	Create a visual format of your child's plan as step 5 in building an education plan.	○	○	○
Chapter 5.	Top of the Class: The New RESP and CESG			
34.	Make an RESP a part of any education savings program.	○	○	○
35.	Understand the basics about RESPs before subscribing to a plan.	○	○	○
36.	Learn to recognize the two types of RESPs.	○	○	○
37.	Consider opting for an individual plan over a family plan.	○	○	○
38.	Understand the four types of withdrawals from an RESP.	○	○	○
39.	Be sure to ask the critical questions before choosing a particular plan.	○	○	○
40.	Choose the subscriber to the RESP carefully.	○	○	○
41.	Make sure your RESP is around for at least 10 years.	○	○	○
42.	Consider postponing RRSP contributions if it looks like your child won't be enrolling in a postsecondary institution.	○	○	○
43.	If your RESP beneficiaries are more than six years apart in age, consider separate plans.	○	○	○
44.	Know your investment options for the RESP.	○	○	○
45.	Be sure to designate a successor subscriber in your will.	○	○	○
46.	Ask for a waiver of penalties if they have been applied.	○	○	○

Tim's Tips	Strategy	Should I Make Note of This?		
		Yes	**No**	**Not Sure**
47.	Understand the basic rules of the CESG.	○	○	○
48.	Contribute $4,000 to an RESP over every two-year period to maximize CESGs.	○	○	○
49.	Watch out for the events that could trigger a requirement to repay the CESG.	○	○	○
50.	Leave your unassisted contributions in the plan.	○	○	○
51.	Spread out your RESP contributions to maximize the CESGs if necessary.	○	○	○
Chapter 6.	The Honour Roll: Other Funding Strategies			
52.	Make use of an in-trust account when an RESP won't be enough.	○	○	○
53.	Consider a family trust when you want complete flexibility in controlling the assets that are being set aside.	○	○	○
54.	Life insurance can work as a savings vehicle, but only if the conditions are right.	○	○	○
55.	If you're already in the workforce, ask your employer to contribute to your education.	○	○	○
56.	Lend money to your adult child through a corporation if you're a business owner.	○	○	○
57.	Pay your child to work in the family business to provide a source of education funding.	○	○	○
58.	Consider using your RRSP assets to fund an education for yourself or your spouse.	○	○	○
Chapter 7.	The Study of Money: Financial Planning for Students			
59.	Monitor your child's spending habits and step in when signs of danger appear.	○	○	○

Tim's Tips	Strategy	Should I Make Note of This?		
		Yes	No	Not Sure
60.	Manage student debt properly to minimize the interest costs and maintain a good credit rating.	○	○	○
61.	Take maximum advantage of all tax credits available to students.	○	○	○
62.	Make the most of an RRSP—even if you're a student.	○	○	○
63.	Put a child to work in order to claim a number of tax benefits.	○	○	○
64.	Invest 10 percent of your take-home pay monthly.	○	○	○
65.	Avoid timing the market by sticking with good quality long-term investments.	○	○	○
66.	Understand the investments you're making, or don't make them at all.	○	○	○
67.	Diversify your investments through asset allocation to minimize risks.	○	○	○

FOREWORD

I can still remember my first day of university like it was yesterday. It wasn't so long ago—September 9, 1985, to be exact. I remember thinking just how expensive it was to pursue a postsecondary education. My tuition cost me $1,150 that year. Books were an extra $300, rent for my basement apartment was $207 a month, and food cost me about $150 a month. The grand total? One year of university education cost me $4,306, plus a few bucks in spending money.

And by the way, my rent was about $200 higher per month than it should have been. The apartment was downright scary. My roommate was even more frightening. Jeremy was not the epitome of cleanliness. One weekend, my mother visited our place. Thinking she would be helpful by cleaning the apartment for us, she picked up the small carpet in the middle of the floor and took it outside to beat it. She was astonished at the amount of dust and dirt that came from the carpet. She was even more astonished when I announced that the carpet was not a carpet at all—it was my roommate's towel. I have fond memories from those days.

While the dirty roommate syndrome is still commonplace on college and university campuses across Canada, the cost of education has not remained static. On the contrary, education costs have skyrocketed since my days in school not so long ago. Today, paying for a child's education in Canada is no small task, which is why I have written this book.

My hope is that by the time you have finished these pages, you will appreciate the importance and magnitude of the task ahead—that is, finding the money for the education of that special child, or children, in your life. And further, that you will have the answers to enable you to make smart decisions about financing that education.

This book is for parents, grandparents, aunts, uncles, friends, neighbours, and anyone else who wants to help a child through postsecondary school. My thanks to you for being concerned about this next generation, who, without question, will need an education to survive in our global economy.

Tim Cestnick, CA, CFP
August 1999

MEETING THE CLASSMATES: THE JOHNSTON FAMILY

If three's a crowd, then twenty-three must be a classroom.

1

Getting to Know the Johnstons

I still remember the countless summer nights when the Johnston family—the *large* Johnston family, who lived next door to my family when I was growing up—would fire up the barbeque, and the smell of chicken and steak would flood our neighbour-hood. I'm getting hungry even as I reminisce about those days. When it came time to sit down and eat those meals, they would push together the picnic table that could seat eight, one of those outdoor plastic patio tables that could seat another six people, and a round patio table for the kids. Aside from the size of the family, this scene doesn't sound so strange. But get this: None of these festivities ever took place in the back yard.

No sir, the front yard was where this family felt most comfortable. And you wouldn't find a more hospitable family anywhere. I think Margaret Johnston wanted to eat in the front yard so that she could flag down passers-by and invite them to dinner. Her husband, Burt, although a little more reserved than Margaret, enjoyed it just as much.

I'd need twenty hands and feet to count the number of meals I've had at the Johnston home. I know I'll never find myself living on a park bench in downtown Toronto, rummaging through garbage for scraps to eat. The Johnstons would adopt me long before that happened. They'd adopt you too. The Johnstons were the most outgoing, flamboyant family in our neighbourhood. Strike that—in all of Oakville. And their home was always the centre of attention. Not surprising, perhaps, for a family that had a pink Cadillac in the driveway. (The car belonged to Margaret.)

Burt and Margaret have five children: Skye, Randy (known as RJ), Judi, Carolyn, and Janice. That's right, four daughters. Those girls turned heads wherever they went, whether they were driving the pink Cadillac or not. Every guy in Oakville knew of the Johnston sisters. Today, all the sisters are married, living across North America from Vancouver to Boston. RJ, the Johnston's only son, was always overshadowed by his sisters, except on the ice where he played pro hockey for a time. Today, he's a successful stockbroker living with his wife and three terrific kids in Alabama.

Today the Johnston home is still a hive of hospitality, even though Burt and Margaret now live there alone. When their kids and grandchildren come home to visit, you'd swear there was some kind of national convention going on in town. Each summer the neighbourhood braces itself for the annual migration of the Johnston clan. July is when Burt and Margaret's kids usually return to Oakville with their spouses and the grandchildren for a visit.

Questioning the Tax Guy

In July last year I found myself in a familiar spot—sitting at a table in the Johnston's front yard eating dinner. Janice, the youngest of Burt and Margaret's kids, who now lives in Langley, British Columbia, was back in town with her husband, Peter, and their three children— Tori, age seven, Lincoln, age five, and Virginia, age three. Carolyn, Burt and Margaret's fourth child, was also there. She still lives in Oakville, and is married with a four-year-old son and a two-year-old daughter.

As usual, Burt was sharing with us his most recent collection of jokes, picked up at his last Rotary Club meeting. Margaret was singing a hymn with the grandkids, and I was sitting there quietly, waiting for the inevitable—a tax question. After all, I'm the "tax guy," and it never fails that someone has something to ask. Don't get me wrong. I really don't mind answering tax questions. The truth is, I enjoy it.

After 40 minutes of jokes, singing, and talking about everything from the Blue Jays to recent movies, no one had asked me a tax question. Finally I couldn't take it any longer. "All right," I said, "how come no one has asked me a question yet?" The table fell silent. I looked around. "Who are you people?" I asked. "And what have you done with the Johnston family?"

"Well, now that you mention it," Peter said, "I do have a few questions about these registered education savings plans everyone is talking about—RESPs, I think they're called. In fact, I happen to have an application form and a few other papers here to ask you about," he continued, as he pulled from under the table a suitcase the likes of which I had seen only once before.

My wife used to have a suitcase just like it. It was so big that when she bought new luggage, I broke the monster in two and made one half into a sandbox for our son Winston and the other half into a wading pool.

"Peter," I asked, "how did you manage to lug that suitcase from B.C.?"

"A forklift at home, flatbed truck to the airport, and Margaret's Cadillac once we arrived in Toronto," Peter replied. "But don't panic, Tim. There's more than just RESP information here. Janice packed the water skis and a volleyball net in here too."

Gathering of the Clan

A couple of days after that meal, the rest of Burt and Margaret's clan arrived. The next to show up, from Richmond, B.C., was Skye with her husband, Randy, five-year-old daughter, Chloe, and two-year-old son, Joshua. Skye is teased as the quiet daughter in the family. She may seem quiet when you first meet her, but don't be fooled. She once won a yodelling competition in Hungary.

Judi was next to arrive. She lives in Boston, and is usually the first to return each year. (She hates to miss out on anything.) Last summer, however, her husband, Ned, had to stay in Boston to finish a book he was writing, something about the Y2K issue. At any rate, Judi and Ned, along with their daughter, Alexi, age nine, and sons Zuri, age six, and Samuel, age two, arrived in plenty of time to experience the Johnston family petting zoo. No, you won't find this zoo in the Johnston's front yard. It's in the back yard, right next to the pool. (Unlike my house, which simply has a wading pool that used to be half a suitcase, Burt has a real in-ground pool.) Burt had stocked the petting zoo with ants, worms, and a couple of frogs. From time to time, the kids find a bear or donkey in the zoo, but only when Burt or one of his sons-in-law can muster the gumption to put on the costumes.

As I said, Burt and Margaret's only son is RJ. RJ, his wife Lisa, and their kids Lindsay, age 15, Logan, age 12, and Jamie Ann, age 10, arrived a day or so after Judi and her family. RJ brings a measure of sanity to the chaos that occurs when all the Johnston offspring descend on Oakville at the same time. He's like the calm in the midst of the storm—the voice of reason.

Knowing Where I Fit In

Yes, the whole Johnston clan was back in town. Later that week, I found myself sitting at the picnic table in their front yard, eating corn on the cob. I came armed with a couple of jokes myself, just for Burt.

"Burt, what's 40 feet long and has 8 teeth?" I asked.

"Don't know," he said.

"The front row at a Willie Nelson concert!" I was laughing hysterically. Burt didn't crack a smile. Turns out he has every album ever released by Willie Nelson. If you're a fan too, no offence.

There was a new face at the table this time. Her name was Janet, a friend of Margaret's. Janet, a single mom with a daughter named Allison, age 15, told me how difficult it has been for her to make ends meet, and she wondered how in the world she was going to pay for Allison's education. We chatted for a bit, then I mentioned that I would be writing this book. I promised to give her a copy and to sit down with her after she'd read it to help her put a plan in place for Allison's education.

Dessert has always been my favourite part of dinner at the Johnston's, and on this night Carolyn had made her specialty—chocolate chip cookies. If there's one culinary benefit I enjoy in life, it's being married to Carolyn. That's right, Burt and Margaret are my father- and mother-in-law. Truthfully, I couldn't be happier than to be part of this crazy, chaotic clan.

Telling You For a Reason

Why would I introduce you to my in-laws? Simple. As you browse the pages of this book, you're going to read examples of how to implement the rules and strategies I propose. To make these examples effective, I needed a family who could serve as guinea pigs, so to speak. I needed a family with older kids, younger kids, aunts, uncles, grandparents, Canadian-resident kids, and non-resident kids; with RESPs and no education plans at all; with members who are employees and those who are self-employed—a family that is generally in need of help on the education savings front. The Johnston family fits the bill. Besides, they'll still love me when I tell them I'm not paying them anything for this little endeavour. Of course, they'll each get a free copy of this book and my appreciation for a lifetime. What more could they want?

MATHEMATICS 101: CALCULATING THE COST OF EDUCATION

It now costs more
to amuse a child than
it did to educate either
of his parents.

2

The date? July 13, last summer. It was my mother-in-law's birthday. Margaret wouldn't tell us her age, but my niece Tori figured it out. She found Grandma's purse and pulled out her driver's licence. "Grandma, I know how old you are!" Tori shouted. "And your licence says you got an 'F' in sex!" Fortunately, Grandma Margaret has a sense of humour.

Grandma Margaret had decided to celebrate this birthday in a different way. After blowing out the candles on her cake, she gave each of her grandchildren a gift of their own. Inside envelopes addressed to each one she had placed a cheque for $500. The catch? She explained that the money was to be used exclusively for their education.

RJ couldn't resist the urge to make a suggestion. "Mom, that's great, that is *really* great. But can't Logan use the cash for something he needs now? He could really use some new golf clubs. And I'd be happy to help him break them in."

Peter stepped in. "I hear that it's going to cost a lot to send our kids to school, so thanks, Margaret." We were all appreciative. And Peter was right. It's going to cost a sizeable sum to send our kids to school. Sure, my kids are very young. We've got 15 years to go before our first child, Winston, pursues a postsecondary education (and he will). It makes sense that it's going to cost more then than it does today.

But what about Janet's daughter, Allison, who is already 15 years old? In just 3 more years she'll be heading for university, and it's going to cost her approximately 175 percent more than it cost me just 15 years ago. She can expect to pay $66,700 for 4 years of university beginning in 2003, since she plans to live away from home. What 18-year-old doesn't want the same? Given the state of her family's financial affairs, however, living at home and going to a university close by might be a more realistic option.

Action Step

The education of that special child in your life is going to be expensive. It used to be that a child and his parents, along with a little help from the government, could easily pay for a postsecondary education. Things are changing—and fast. It's time for grandparents to enter the picture. Families will need to rely on grandma and grandpa as at no other time in the past to help with education costs. If you're a grandparent, talk over the education issue with your own kids to determine how you might be able to help your grandkids get the education they're going to need.

Even then, she can expect to pay $42,686 for a 4-year university education. Not exactly chump change.

Rising Education Costs

Regardless of when the children in your life expect to attend postsecondary school, the costs may be more than you think.

Tim's Tip 1: Avoid unpleasant surprises when it comes time to cut the first tuition cheque.

Canadians remain in the dark when it comes to understanding how much it's going to cost to send their kids to school. According to a telephone survey done by the Bank of Montreal in July 1997,
- 42 percent of parents in Canada estimate that a 4-year university or college education will cost less than $50,000 in 18 years' time and
- 13 percent have no idea what it will cost.

The truth is, in 18 years' time a 4-year university education is expected to cost between $112,295 and $149,709, depending on whether or not the child lives at home while attending school.

The same Bank of Montreal survey revealed that 58 percent of parents have started to save for their child's education, but that one quarter of these parents have saved less than $1,000, with the median savings at $1,600. A full 40 percent of all parents, including those who haven't set aside any education savings yet, are "extremely confident" or "very confident" that they will save enough to pay for most or all of their child's education. Sounds optimistic to me.

Here's what I mean: If these parents were to invest the median figure of $1,600 annually for 18 years, earning an average annual return of 8 percent, they'd end up with $64,714 by the time their child is ready to darken the doors of a university or college. Don't forget, the young student is likely to need in the neighbourhood of

$112,295 to make it through school. So, although mom and dad thought they were doing enough, they're facing a shortfall of over $47,000.

I'm not suggesting it's mom and dad's responsibility to pay for 100 percent of their child's education. But the onus is on all parents to know how much they plan to contribute to their child's education and to have some notion of how the balance of the necessary funds will be raised. In other words, it's the job of all parents, as a minimum, to avoid unpleasant surprises when it comes time for that first tuition cheque to be cut.

TO MAKE A LONG STORY SHORT:

- Over 40 percent of parents underestimate what it will cost 18 years from now to send a child to a postsecondary institution for 4 years.

- Of the 58 percent who have started saving for their child's education, more than half have saved less than $1,600.

- The onus is on parents to avoid being surprised when it comes time to pay the bills for education.

Did You Know?

Ponder these statistics: Since 1987, the increases in university tuition costs have been greater than the annual inflation rate in every year. In fact, tuition fees have risen by 138 percent since 1987, while the cost of living has increased by just 28 percent, according to Statistics Canada. Since 1992, tuition costs have risen by 56 percent, while the overall rise in consumer prices was just 6 percent. And check this out: tuition costs have increased by an average annual rate of 9.06 percent since 1987.

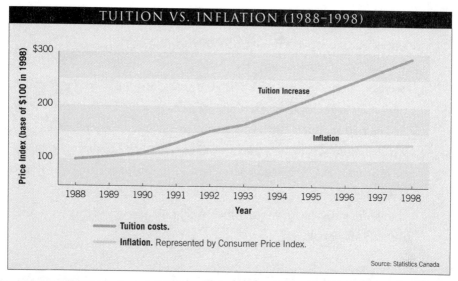

	Canada	Newfoundland	Prince Edward Island	Nova Scotia	New Brunswick	Québec	Ontario	Manitoba	Saskatchewan	Alberta	British Columbia
UNDERGRADUATE ARTS TUITION (1990–1997)											
1990	$1,438	$1,353	$1,863	$1,962	$1,842	$909	$1,638	$1,497	$1,539	$1,322	$1,684
1991	$1,681	$1,554	$2,120	$2,221	$1,998	$1,307	$1,779	$1,726	$1,828	$1,520	$1,868
1992	$1,823	$1,709	$2,298	$2,441	$2,206	$1,445	$1,906	$2,002	$2,065	$1,786	$1,886
1993	$1,991	$1,993	$2,484	$2,692	$2,338	$1,548	$2,035	$2,109	$2,282	$2,169	$2,077
1994	$2,178	$2,149	$2,623	$2,945	$2,355	$1,689	$2,239	$2,222	$2,447	$2,446	$2,249
1995	$2,333	$2,312	$2,820	$3,172	$2,496	$1,694	$2,458	$2,338	$2,591	$2,708	$2,366
1996	$2,867	$2,670	$2,920	$3,499	$2,769	$1,725	$2,936	$2,505	$2,239	$2,955	$2,661
1997	$3,117	$3,150	$3,150	$3,737	$2,992	$1,726	$3,234	$2,593	$2,380	$3,211	$2,705

Tim's Tip 2: **Understand the trend of education costs over the last decade.**

You have to take a close look at how education costs have changed over the last decade to really appreciate where they are headed over the next few years. Since a picture is worth a thousand words, you might be interested in seeing the rise in tuition costs relative to overall consumer prices, as measured by the Consumer Price Index. Check out the tables on the previous page.

Okay, let me throw some hard numbers at you. Back in 1987, average tuition fees were $1,310. Ten years later, in 1997, those same tuition fees set a student back $3,117. That's some kind of increase!

The bottom line? The trend is toward higher education costs, which should serve as a wake-up call to Canadian families who may be hoping to help their kids purchase an education. It's time for families to make plans to win the education savings game. These plans should include several tools, which we'll talk about more as we walk through this book.

TO MAKE A LONG STORY SHORT:

- Between 1987 and 1997, tuition costs rose by 138 percent, compared to increases in overall consumer prices of just 28 percent.

- This increase in tuition costs represents an average annual increase of 9.06 percent.

- It's time for families to make plans to win the education savings game, using tools that I'll talk about in this book.

Tim's Tip 3: **Watch for signs that education costs will continue to soar.**

In my mind, two key indicators—government cutbacks in funding for postsecondary institutions and rising enrollment figures—point to one conclusion: Education costs will continue to increase at a rate consistent with the rate of the last decade.

Government Cutbacks

Talk to the vice-president of finance of any college or university in Canada and you'll hear the same song. It's a little ditty called

"Gimme Back My Funding." It's not exactly a chart-topper at the Department of Finance.

Want proof that schools have been losing out on the funding front? Statistics Canada stated in a 1980 report that tuition fees made up just 13 percent of universities' general operating revenues at that time. In 1995, tuition fees accounted for an average of almost 30 percent of those revenues. In fact, tuition fees cover a wide-ranging share of the costs at different universities—from 15 percent at

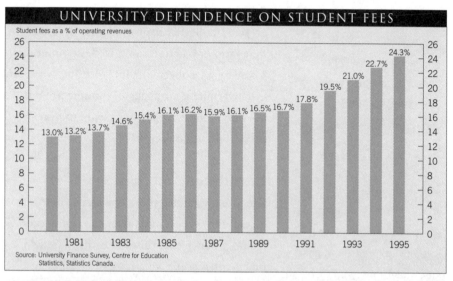

UNIVERSITY DEPENDENCE ON STUDENT FEES

Student fees as a % of operating revenues

13.0% 13.2% 13.7% 14.6% 15.4% 16.1% 16.2% 15.9% 16.1% 16.5% 16.7% 17.8% 19.5% 21.0% 22.7% 24.3%

Source: University Finance Survey, Centre for Education Statistics, Statistics Canada.

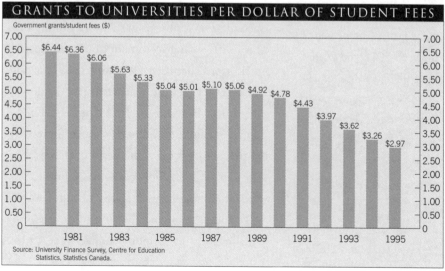

GRANTS TO UNIVERSITIES PER DOLLAR OF STUDENT FEES

Government grants/student fees ($)

$6.44 $6.36 $6.06 $5.63 $5.33 $5.04 $5.01 $5.10 $5.06 $4.92 $4.78 $4.43 $3.97 $3.62 $3.26 $2.97

Source: University Finance Survey, Centre for Education Statistics, Statistics Canada.

universities in Québec, where tuition fees are the lowest in the country, to over 40 percent at universities that charge higher fees.

There's no doubt about it, we're moving towards an American-style education system in which the student is expected to pick up the tab for the lion's share of the cost of his education. The table on the previous page shows that back in 1980 universities received $6.44 in grants from the government for every $1 collected from students. By 1995 that ratio had deteriorated to $2.97 in grants for every $1 collected from students.

Government cutbacks in funding are not the only indicator that increasing tuition costs are here to stay.

Enrollment Increases

I've already talked about the significant increase in tuition costs over the last decade. It's no wonder that tuition has increased so much when you take a look at enrollment numbers. The fact is that enrollment in post-secondary institutions grew more rapidly in the 1980s than government grants to those institutions. Between 1980 and 1989, government grants grew, in real terms (that is, after inflation is factored in), by 11 percent. Full-time-equivalent enrollment, however, grew by 38 percent over the same period. The result? The shortfall in funding was passed on to students in the form of higher tuition fees.

Despite the big increase in tuition fees, enrollment rates for both younger (age 19 to

Did You Know?

The percentage of 19- to 24-year-olds enrolled in university rose every year from 1980 to 1995. The enrollment rate of this group rose from 10 percent in 1980 to 18.6 percent in 1995. Sure, the number of young people in this age group has declined over the same period, but the higher enrollment rate more than compensated for the fewer number of young people. Between 1976 and 1995, the enrollment rate for 19- to 24-year olds grew by 50 percent. What about those over age 24? You might be surprised to learn that enrollment rates for those aged 25 to 34 increased by a whopping 120 percent between 1976 and 1995.

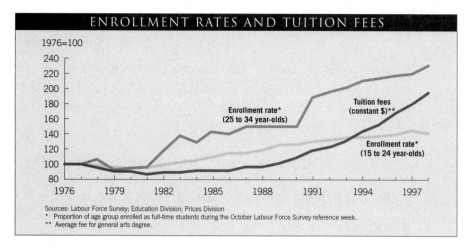

ENROLLMENT RATES AND TUITION FEES

1976=100

Enrollment rate*
(25 to 34 year-olds)

Tuition fees
(constant $)**

Enrollment rate*
(15 to 24 year-olds)

1976 1979 1982 1985 1988 1991 1994 1997

Sources: Labour Force Survey; Education Division; Prices Division
* Proportion of age group enrolled as full-time students during the October Labour Force Survey reference week.
** Average fee for general arts degree.

24) and older (age 25 to 34) full-time students have continued to rise. A logical explanation is that students recognize that job prospects are much better for those with an education.

The bottom line? Government funding and enrollment rates have a lot to do with the price tag of a postsecondary education. As a higher percentage of the population recognizes the importance of an education and enrolls in Canada's colleges and universities, and as government grants fail to keep pace with this increase due to the pressure to avoid deficits, education costs will continue to rise. Sorry for the bad news, folks.

TO MAKE A LONG STORY SHORT:

- Government grants to colleges and universities, and enrollment rates, have a lot to do with the cost of education.

- Government grants have been on the decline relative to enrollments, which have been increasing. The result? Higher tuition fees charged to students to cover the shortfall.

- This trend is likely to continue.

Comparing Canada and the World

It's a good idea to examine where Canadian tuition costs are in relation to average tuition costs in other countries. It will give you a perspective you may not have had before.

Tim's Tip 4: Compare our tuition fees to those in other countries to understand where we are globally.

My brother-in-law Ned (Judi's husband) is a chess fanatic. I always get a kick out of watching Ned and Peter (Janice's husband) go at it at the chess board. Neither of them likes to lose. The tension in the room when these two meet over chess is thick enough to cut with a knife, and you'd swear, from the sweat on their brows, that they were playing in the seventh game of the Stanley Cup finals. Ned beat Peter this time, and now he had to face a somewhat less formidable foe—me.

As we pondered our moves, Ned talked to me about, among other things, the cost of education in the United States. "Ned, I'm trying to concentrate," I finally said. "You could at least pretend that this is a challenging game of chess—you know, to boost my waning self-confidence."

"Checkmate," Ned announced. "Good game, Tim. Now, about those education costs. I've heard that tuition fees in the United States are higher than they are in Canada."

Ned was right. Tuition costs south of the border are generally higher than they are here. And it concerned Ned. After all, Ned, Judi, and their kids live in Boston, the education capital of the States.

You might think that as Canadians we have it pretty good as far as tuition costs are concerned. This might be true in comparison to the United States, but when you look at the other member countries of the Organization for Economic Cooperation and Development (OECD), we

EDUCATION FEES AMONG OECD COUNTRIES (1997)		
Country	User Fees (in Canadian dollars)	National System of Grants
Australia	Yes – $1,832	Yes
Austria	No	Yes
Belgium	Yes – $1000	Yes
Canada	Yes – $3,117	No
Czech Republic	No	Yes
Denmark	No	Yes
Finland	No	Yes
France	No	Yes
Germany	No	Yes
Greece	No	Yes
Hungary	No	Yes
Iceland	No	Yes
Ireland	No	Yes
Italy	Yes – $500	Yes
Japan	Yes – $4,000	No
Luxembourg	not available	not available
Mexico	No	Yes
New Zealand	Yes – $1,760	Yes
Norway	No	Yes
Portugal	Yes	Yes
Spain	Yes – $1,500	Yes
Sweden	No	Yes
Switzerland	Yes – $800	Yes
The Netherlands	No	Yes
Turkey	No	Yes
United Kingdom	No – $1,500 in 1998	Yes
United States	Yes – $4,060	Yes
Source: Canadian Federation of Students		

don't fare so well. The table on the previous page shows the average one-year undergraduate tuition fees in an arts program, by country, at a public institution equivalent to a Canadian university, for the 1997 school year.

A fact sheet published by the Canadian Federation of Students explains that in May 1976 Canada signed the United Nations' International Covenant on Economic, Social, and Cultural Rights. Under Part 3 of Article 13, *Right to Education*, subsection 2(c) reads: "Higher education shall be made equally accessible to all, on the basis of capacity, by every appropriate means, and in particular by the progressive introduction of free education."

Free education? Sounds good to me. But try holding the federal government to that promise, made over 20 years ago! The table, however, shows that more than half of all OECD countries have lived up to the promise of free education. Of those that do levy tuition fees, only Japan and the United States have higher average fees than Canada.

TO MAKE A LONG STORY SHORT:

- In 1976, Canada signed a United Nations covenant in which our government promised to progressively introduce free education.

- In spite of this promise, tuition costs have increased significantly since that time, and only Japan and the United States now have higher average tuition costs than Canada.

- My brother-in-law Ned is a chess fanatic.

Forecasting Future Education Costs

You've seen the history of education costs and where we stand relative to other OECD countries. The big question, of course, is, what will it cost to send my child to postsecondary school when that time comes?

Tim's Tip 5: **Don't distinguish between college and university costs when planning for the future.**

You're probably thinking that I've been throwing around stats on the costs of education, but I haven't differentiated between college and university costs. Traditionally there has been a difference between college and university costs in Canada. College costs have generally been lower, partly because college programs have been shorter in duration (two- and three-year programs are common), colleges pay their instructors less than university instructors earn, and colleges don't have to fund research to the extent universities do. My advice to you is, don't distinguish between college and university costs when planning for your child's education. Make the assumption that university rates will apply.

I spoke at length on this topic with the former vice-president of finance at Sheridan College in Oakville, Ontario— Kathryn Cestnick. Yes, she's related to me. She's my mother. She has been immersed in the Canadian college system for more years than she'll allow me to disclose— without jeopardizing my inheritance, that is. Having held very senior positions at three community colleges in Ontario, she knows a thing or two about college tuition fees.

She advised me that in Ontario college fees were deregulated in 1998. Deregulation has opened the door for Ontario colleges to increase tuition fees to

Don't make the mistake of assuming that in the future a year of college education will cost your child less than a year of university education. If you estimate a college education to cost less, your reason should be that the educational program at college will not take as long to complete, and not because college tuition costs per year differ from those at universities. Keep in mind, too, that many college programs today do in fact take as long as an undergraduate university degree.

Caution!

whatever the market will bear, provided the program is in demand and work is available in the field of study. As a result, certain college programs could become more expensive than similar programs at a university. At Sheridan College, for example, the animation program is so popular that you'd have to pay more to enroll in it than you would for a typical arts degree at a university.

Don't be surprised if other provinces follow Ontario's example and deregulate college tuition fees. While some colleges may view access to education as a key factor in their success, and as a result they may keep a lid on the cost of education, many colleges will begin charging tuition fees that look more like university fees. The point here is that when planning for a child's education, it's no longer appropriate to distinguish between college and university costs. Plan for one level of expected costs—those consistent with attendance at a university.

TO MAKE A LONG STORY SHORT:

- I have not distinguished between college and university costs in the statistics I have cited—and for good reason.

- College fees across the country are undergoing a process of deregulation, and you can expect many college and university programs to cost about the same in the future.

Tim's Tip 6: Consider when, where, and how your child will attend school when calculating the cost of your child's education.

It's time to get down to the nitty-gritty of determining how much it's likely to cost your child to attend a postsecondary school. Several costs should be factored into the grand total. I've listed them below, giving the average costs for these items in 1999:

AVERAGE COST 1999	
Tuition and ancillary fees	$3,403
Books and supplies	$1,200
Accommodation	$3,200
Food	$1,400
Transportation	$1,000
Personal care	$1,500
Recreation and entertainment	$1,200
Total average cost for one year	**$12,903**

These figures were provided by Human Resources Development Canada, except the tuition figure, which I obtained from Statistics Canada. If you're able to get a good handle on what these items are likely to cost, then you'll manage to avoid any unpleasant surprises when it comes time for your child to hit the books. These costs, however, can vary, depending on when, where, and how your child goes to school. Here's what I mean:

When Is Your Child Going to School?

It makes sense that if your child is heading to school in just two years, the costs associated with his education will be less than for a child who won't be going for another 15 years. The reason is inflation. You've probably heard of it.

Of course, we can make different assumptions about the rate of inflation on the costs I've listed above. For example, will accommodation costs increase by 1 percent, 5 percent, or somewhere in between over the next number of years? Using an inflation estimate of 3 percent for the non-tuition costs above makes a lot of sense, given historical rates of inflation. Most economists would agree that this is a reasonable assumption.

But what about tuition costs? This one is a little tougher. We've seen average annual increases in tuition of 9.06 percent over the last decade. There's no doubt that the trend for tuition costs will continue to move upward, but at this same annual clip of 9.06 percent? Possibly. It only makes sense, then, to do your calculations assuming a rate of return consistent with this figure. I've used 9 percent for tuition inflation. You'll find the numbers in Appendix A at the back of the book.

I know some of you will disagree with me about the 9 percent inflation. For your benefit, I've also done the calculations assuming 7 percent and 5 percent rates of tuition inflation. As for me, I'm assuming 9 percent annual increases when planning for the future of my kids.

Where Is Your Child Going to School?

Some schools are more expensive than others. That's just the way life is. My niece Lindsay, RJ's oldest daughter, is 15 years old this year. She recently announced that she plans to attend Harvard Business School in three years.

"Any idea what that will cost each year?" I asked her.

"Not really," she said, "but I'm working part-time at the movie theatre, so I'll be able to save enough, I think."

"Lindsay, I'm sure you'll earn enough at the theatre to go to Harvard, if that's what you want. But you'd better plan on working there until you're about—oh, I'd say 63. If you're lucky, Harvard might have easier entrance requirements for seniors."

The cost of education at an American college or university varies greatly—

Action Step

There's no place like home—to save big bucks when enrolled at a postsecondary institution. If money is tight, encourage your child to live at home and enroll at a school she can commute to. The savings can be as much as $40,000 over a four-year program if your child stays at home. If she insists on living away from home, help keep costs to a minimum by sending her food at least monthly, where your distance from the school makes this practical, rather than encouraging her to buy it at school. And most important—rather than accepting long-distance phone charges, teach your child to use smoke signals.

depending on its reputation and prestige as well as whether it's a state or private institution. In Canada, if you're planning to attend a publicly funded school, there's not much discrepancy between the cost of an education at one school and another. The figures in Appendix A are averages across Canada and should do the trick in helping you assess the costs your child will face in the future.

How Is Your Child Going to School?

Is the child in your life planning to live at home during those postsec-ondary years, or will he live at school? Don't be surprised if your child decides that living at school is cool. It *is* cool. There's nothing quite like living on your own for the first time. You may recall your own school days.

Ah yes, a 900-square-foot shack called home by seven first-year students. The relentless smell of mold, and green stuff growing in the fridge. Tenants averaging four hours sleep a night, except on week-ends, when everyone sleeps in until 1 p.m. And those are the *advan-tages* of living away from home.

The disadvantages? It costs more money. You'll notice that Appendix A is in two parts: one estimate for those who plan to live away from home, and another for those who will live at home (where the food and general cleanliness are of a higher quality).

For those of you who want to be spared the details, there's a sum-mary of the total costs you'll find in Appendix A on the next page.

Now, compare the costs if your child decides to shun the "socially preferred" option of living at school and stays at home. The differ-ence between the figures below and the ones above is that accommo-dation and food costs are removed from the calculation.

TO MAKE A LONG STORY SHORT:

- The cost of your child's education will depend largely on when your child will be attending school, which school he will attend, and whether or not he'll be living at home.

- Appendix A in the back of the book details the expected costs of education based on different assumptions about inflation.

EXPECTED EDUCATION COSTS: LIVING AWAY FROM HOME				
First Year of School	Tuition Fees	Other Costs	Total Costs	Expected Cost for Four Years
2000	$3,709	$9,785	$13,494	$57,900
2002	4,407	10,381	14,788	63,584
2004	5,236	11,013	16,249	70,019
2006	6,221	11,684	17,905	77,329
2008	7,391	12,395	19,786	85,657
2010	8,781	13,150	21,931	95,173
2012	10,433	13,951	24,384	106,077
2014	12,395	14,801	27,196	118,606
2016	14,727	15,702	30,429	133,040
2018	17,497	16,658	34,155	149,709

EXPECTED EDUCATION COSTS: LIVING AT HOME				
First Year of School	Tuition Fees	Other Costs	Total Costs	Expected Cost for Four Years
2000	$3,709	$4,532	$8,241	$35,923
2002	4,407	4,808	9,215	40,269
2004	5,236	5,101	10,337	45,284
2006	6,221	5,411	11,632	51,088
2008	7,391	5,741	13,132	57,818
2010	8,781	6,091	14,872	65,638
2012	10,433	6,462	16,894	74,744
2014	12,395	6,855	19,250	85,365
2016	14,727	7,273	21,999	97,774
2018	17,497	7,715	25,212	112,295

Recognizing the Importance of Education

After digesting the figures above, you may be thinking: "Who needs a postsecondary education anyway? I know lots of people who have done well enough for themselves without any formal education. What's the big deal?"

Okay, just how important is a postsecondary education to the well-being of your child?

Tim's Tip 7: Understand that a higher percentage of jobs each year will require a postsecondary education.

The federal Department of Finance has said that by the year 2000 a full 65 percent of all new jobs in Canada will require a postsecondary education (Source: *Agenda Jobs and Growth: A New Framework for Economic Policy*, October 1994). This statistic might just be enough to scare high school dropouts into taking a closer look at their future. A student who is thinking about skipping college or university might want to think again. Check out the competition as shown by the table on the following page.

This table has some interesting things to say. For example, if you were a man of working age back in 1970 looking for a new job, 57.6 percent of those in the work-force (your competition) would have had a

Your attitude towards education as a parent, grandparent, or guardian is going to have a significant effect on how that child in your life values postsecondary school. Make sure you carefully monitor the attitudes, values, and information you feed to that child. And as far as I'm concerned, *no* signal to your child about postsecondary school is as hurtful as a negative signal. Your child might have survived 10 years ago without an education, but he'll be behind the eight ball without an education in the new millennium.

Caution!

COMPOSITION OF THE CANADIAN WORKFORCE (FULL-TIME EMPLOYEES, AGED 25 TO 29)		
Women	**1970**	**1995**
high school or less	61.7%	23.9%
postsecondary non–completers	11.0%	9.0%
postsecondary certificate/diploma	18.0%	40.2%
university graduates	9.3%	26.9%
men	**1970**	**1995**
high school or less	57.6%	34.3%
postsecondary non–completers	10.1%	8.1%
postsecondary certificate/diploma	20.0%	35.8%
university graduates	12.3%	21.9%

Sources: 1970: Statistics Canada, Census of Canada, microdata file.
1995: Statistics Canada, Survey of Consumer Finance, microdata file.

high school education or less. Just 12.3 percent were university graduates.

Now check out the change in those stats as of 1995. A man looking for a job in 1995 was facing this kind of competition: 35.8 percent of his (male) competitors had a postsecondary certificate or diploma, and 21.9 percent had graduated from university. This means that a full 57.7 percent of men in the workforce in 1995 had completed some type of postsecondary education.

That's the competition.

The percentages are even higher for women—a full 67.1 percent of women in the workforce in 1995 had completed postsecondary education.

Make no mistake, the competition gets tougher each year as the percentage of those in the workforce with a postsecondary education increases.

TO MAKE A LONG STORY SHORT:

• The Department of Finance says that 65 percent of all new jobs in the year 2000 will require a postsecondary education.

- The competition in the job market is likely to be educated. In fact, 57.7 percent of all men and 67.1 percent of all women in the workforce in 1995 had completed postsecondary education.

Tim's Tip 8: Understand that unemployment rates for those with a postsecondary education are much lower than for those without.

You know, the Canadian economy went through a rough ride in the early 1990s. Despite this, the employment prospects for those with a postsecondary education have remained very good. Consider those who completed college or university between 1976 and 1995. Specifically, let's look at unemployment rates for youth aged 20 to 24, based on level of education, over that time period. The unem-

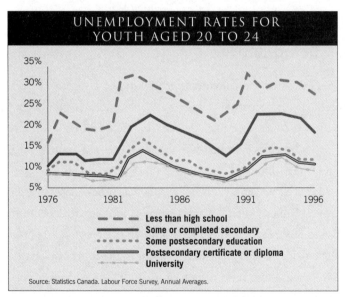

ployment rate of university-educated 20- to 24-year-olds has followed the ups and downs of the general labour market, but it has not shown an upward trend. I can't say the same for those with a high school education only. Check out the graph above:

The graph is pretty clear: Obtain a postsecondary education and you're likely to remain off the welfare rolls. Over time, more and more of those who do not have an education will find themselves out of work.

TO MAKE A LONG STORY SHORT:

• The percentage of postsecondary graduates aged 20 to 24 who are unemployed has remained consistent over time, in line with the general unemployment rate, a reasonable (for Canada) rate of approximately 8 percent.

• Over time, a greater percentage of those without an education will find themselves unemployed.

Tim's Tip 9: Check out the expected rate of return from a postsecondary education. It can be attractive.

Have you ever stopped to wonder what kind of return on investment your child can expect from a university education? It may seem strange, but it is possible to calculate the rate of return from a college or university education, much like you calculate the returns on your investment portfolio.

In a March 1999 report written for the Canadian Centre for Policy Alternatives, Robert Allen, a professor of economics at the University of British Columbia, presented a breakdown of expected rates of return for specific fields of study. Check them out in the following chart.

In a nutshell, these rates of return were calculated by adding up the costs of obtaining an education (including those costs I set out in Tim's Tip 6) plus the salary or wages that a student forgoes as a result of studying full-time. This amount was then compared to the higher earnings that come as a result of obtaining an education.

It's interesting to note that a postsecondary education benefits a woman even more than it does a man. It's not that women earn more than men when they complete their education, but that they are paid that much less than men when they don't obtain a postsecondary education.

It's also worth noting that according to Allen, the financial benefits to a man of a humanities degree are virtually non-existent. That is, in the past, a man was able to earn just as much by working full-time following high school as he could by going to university and obtaining a humanities degree. Having said this, Allen goes on to make the comment that, where the humanities degree is followed by additional training (such as a teaching degree), the financial value of the humanities degree increases.

RATES OF RETURN FOR UNIVERSITY FIELDS OF STUDY				
	men		women	
	1991	1996	1991	1996
fine arts	n/a	n/a	6.5%	11.9%
humanities	none	none	6.9%	12.2%
social science	13.2%	11.6%	13.4%	17.6%
commerce	11.4%	10.4%	12.9%	17.2%
agriculture/biology	4.9%	5.0%	7.1%	11.7%
engineering	14.3%	12.3%	10.7%	14.6%
other health	5.6%	5.6%	15.0%	18.1%
nursing	n/a	n/a	11.5%	15.3%
physical science	7.7%	7.4%	11.4%	15.3%
education	5.5%	5.6%	11.8%	17.6%
humanities/education	8.1%	7.7%	7.6%	9.6%

Notes: For all fields except humanities/educ. the rates of return are based on the earnings of someone with a bachelor degree in the indicated field but with no further university education compared to a high school graduate (grade 12) with no further education.

For humanities/educ. the rates of return are based on the earnings of someone with a bachelor degree education but with no further university education compared to a high school graduate (grade 12) with no further education. It is presumed that the university program takes five years instead of four.

Source: Prof. Robert Allen, University of British Columbia

Let me add this in closing: Aside from the economic benefits of a college or university education, there are intangible benefits that are tough to quantify. I'm talking about a stronger sense of self-esteem, increased confidence, a broader perspective on life, and the abilities to think, to comprehend, and to express oneself. You know, all that other stuff that should not be forgotten.

TO MAKE A LONG STORY SHORT:

- The rate of return on a postsecondary education can be attractive, even more so for women than for men.

- A humanities degree in the hands of a man is not as valuable as other degrees, unless it is followed up with additional training.

- A college or university education brings lots of intangible benefits too.

WINNING THE EDUCATION SAVINGS GAME

Action Step

For the best job opportunities, encourage your child to pursue education that provides very practical and marketable skills—you know, things like dentistry, nursing, accounting, or computer science. And if your child is not cut out for anything so obviously practical, but would rather study history, sociology, or the like, encourage her to identify those career opportunities that require the skills she is acquiring and to pursue additional training for those careers if necessary.

If you hope to win the education savings game, be sure to follow my advice in this chapter: Don't allow the costs of education to take you by surprise. The onus is on you to think through how the kids in your life will pay for school. Recognize the upward trend of tuition fees and the likelihood that this trend will continue. Calculate the expected education costs for the kids in your life. And finally, understand the importance of a postsecondary education to the well-being of your kids. Refer to the Education Planning Tip Sheet at the front of the book to make note of the tips in this chapter you want to remember or take action on.

ECONOMICS 101:
PAYING FOR
AN EDUCATION

If a man empties his purse
into his head, no one can
take it from him.
                    —Benjamin Franklin

3

Chances are pretty good that if you've read Chapter 2, you'd agree on a couple of things. First, your child's education won't be cheap, unless she enrolls in the school of hard knocks—which I understand is fairly inexpensive but doesn't look as good on a resume as, say, a degree from the University of Toronto, Queen's University, the University of British Columbia, or that small institution down Boston-way called Harvard. Second, despite the high cost of education, an education is critically important.

So you have a dilemma. How is your child going to find enough money to make it through school? Good question. Fortunately, there *is* an answer, but it may not be the same answer for everyone.

Tim's Tip 10: Look at a variety of ways to pay for your child's education.

No single approach is right for everyone. Surprised by this statement? You see, the approach that you choose to meet the costs of educating your child will depend on the type of education your child is looking for, your financial resources, the length of time before your child attends postsecondary school, and your values, among other things.

Here are some examples of what I mean:

Logan has decided that he wants to be a medical doctor. Last time RJ (Logan's father) checked, the cost of attending medical school was higher than for obtaining a three-year arts degree. While Logan is only 12 years old, RJ and his wife, Lisa, will need at some point to closely examine the likelihood that Logan will follow through on his decision to become a doctor. Since RJ and Lisa are able to set aside the money necessary for the education of their kids, they plan to wait until Lindsay, Logan, and Jamie Ann are within two years of high school graduation to assess whether they need to set aside more to cover the costs of the kids' education.

Janet intends to do all she can to help her daughter, Allison, make it through university. Since Allison is already 15 years old, Janet doesn't have a lot of time to put a plan in place. Janet knows that she doesn't have much in the way of financial resources to pay for Allison's schooling, so she will need to look at alternative sources of funding, including scholarships, loans,

and employment for Allison to help pay Allison's way through
school.

S *kye and Randy are parents to Chloe and Joshua, both under*
six years of age. While the couple has enough time to set
aside money for the education of their children, and they plan to
do this, they have decided that it's important to them that their
kids pay for as much of their own education as possible. Their
plan then is to calculate how much they think the kids' education
will cost, and use this information to estimate what percentage
they think the kids can and should pay. Skye and Randy will pro-
vide the rest.

The moral of these stories is that funding the education of your
child can be done in a number of ways: by begging, borrowing, stealing, sweating, and saving. It's critical that you determine today the
approach you're going to take. This chapter has been designed to
give you some guidance in this area. In the next chapter, you'll actually document your plan.

TO MAKE A LONG STORY SHORT:

- There are several ways to pay for a child's education: by begging,
  borrowing, stealing, sweating, and saving.

- The approach you take will depend on the type of education your child is
  looking for, your financial resources, the length of time before your child
  attends a postsecondary school, and your values, among other things.

Begging For Education

Don't worry, I'm not about to suggest that your child take a trip downtown and beg on a street corner. But I do suggest that "free money" is one option to pay for at least a portion of your child's postsecondary education. Free money is money that your child

SOURCES OF FREE MONEY FOR EDUCATION			
	Scholarships and Awards	**Grants and Bursaries**	**Fellowships and Stipends**
What is it?	Funds to cover educational costs.	Funds to cover educational costs.	Funds for specific research areas or academic fields of study.
Who qualifies?	Normally based on academic achievement, community involvement or special skills.	Normally based on financial need.	Restrictive. Those with academic achievement in specific areas.
Where do we find it?	Civic organizations, employers, colleges and universities, individual donors.	Colleges and universities, the government (CESG and CSLP), private organizations.	Government agencies, private foundations, colleges and universities.
How much will it be?	Varies. Most are small ($500 to $1,000).	Most are small amounts.	Can be large amounts.
How long will it last?	Most are annual. Some are renewable.	Most are annual. Some are renewable.	Varies by funding and nature of the project.
Is it taxed?	Taxable. Only the first $500 excluded. Certain "prescribed" prizes will be tax-free.	Taxable. Only the first $500 is excluded.	Taxable. Costs incurred during research may be deductible from this income.

"begs" for, and will never have to repay. Specifically, I'm referring to scholarships, awards, grants, bursaries, fellowships, and stipends— but since that's a mouthful, I call it free money.

Access to free money often involves applications, and sometimes essays and interviews. Of course, that downtown street corner might also pay for a book or two, but let's plan to avoid that option.

Tim's Tip 11: Start thinking about free money well ahead of time, not at the last minute.

Thinking about free money ahead of time should result in two things:
- early involvement
- early application.

Early Involvement

Scholarships and awards are usually handed out on the basis of academic achievement, community involvement, and special skills (such as athletic ability, although athletic scholarships are more prevalent in the United States than in Canada). Students should start thinking about these skills and achievements early in high school.

It's not likely to be enough that your child volunteers in the community or takes up athletic training in a particular sport in his last year of high school. The process should start in the first year of high school. Encourage your child to be actively involved in extra-curricular activities from grade 9 onward. The fact is, academic achievement in the last two

Caution!

There's no doubt about it, finding free money will be hard work. It will take lots of initiative on your part, and on the part of your child. Whatever you do, don't wait until the last minute to look for free money because finding it could take some time, and the deadlines to apply for these funds usually fall well before the academic year the funds are intended to pay for. Chances are pretty good that if you're not looking for free money a year ahead of time, your child won't receive any!

years of high school is what matters most as far as acceptance to postsecondary schools is concerned. This means that the early years of high school are ideal for developing your child's other interests and activities.

Early Application

You know the saying: The early bird catches the worm. This advice is critical when applying for free money. Regardless of whether your child is pursuing scholarships, awards, grants, bursaries, fellowships, or stipends (research grants), get your application in early, since private and institutional money is often awarded on a first-come, first-served basis. Make sure you do your homework to determine the deadlines for filing applications, where applications are necessary.

TO MAKE A LONG STORY SHORT:

- Start your child thinking about free money well in advance of postsecondary school through involvement in extra-curricular activities early in a high school career, and by applying for free money well in advance of the first year of postsecondary education.

- Take the time to learn the deadlines for important applications.

Tim's Tip 12: **Know where to look for free money.**

Finding free money will take some work. The good news? Thousands of potential scholarships, awards, bursaries, and grants are out there for the picking. You and your child should start looking for free money by approaching a high school guidance counsellor early (12 months prior to attending college or university) to find out about any local scholarships or the like that might be available and to check out deadlines for applying for various scholarships and awards.

Next, it's a good idea to approach your employer. You might be surprised at the number of companies with free money to give away to the children of employees—or to employees themselves—for education.

Don't forget to approach the various colleges and universities your child is interested in attending. Most schools offer free money in one form or another.

Finally, I highly recommend that you pick up a copy of a book called *Scholarship* by Brian Harris. This book lists hundreds of scholarships available across the country. It is published by Canadian Guidance Services, 2042 Coral Crescent, Burlington, ON L7P 3K5. You can also order it by hopping on the Internet and visiting the site www.worldchat.com/commercial/canguide/index.html.

When you're looking for free money, consider that your child might be eligible for funds that are earmarked for specific types of students, such as these offerings:

- *Cultural background.* Many groups offer scholarships and the like to students who come from certain cultural or ethnic backgrounds. If your family has a distinct cultural background, it may be worth looking to some of these groups.
- *Memberships.* If you or your family are members of a specific church, social, or recreational group, check to see if the organization offers scholarships or awards to students. It's worth asking.
- *Field of study.* Is your child entering a particular area of study that might draw support from individuals, private foundations, or corporations? Consider this avenue particularly if your child is pursuing a specific profession or occupation. Call the local, municipal, or provincial association for that profession or occupation to enquire about free money.
- *Special needs or disabilities.* If your child possesses a special need or is disabled in some manner, financial help may be available through the government or an association related to the special need or disability.

- *Athletics and the arts.* Perhaps your child possesses a special ability in a particular sport, or in music, drama, dance, or a similar discipline. If this is the case, look for free money from colleges and universities that may recognize your child's talent and want your child to attend their school. Funds could also be available through an association related to the sport or other discipline in which your child excels.

- *Employers.* I've mentioned this one before, but it's worth mentioning again. Check with your employer to determine if any special awards are offered to students who are related to employees of the company.

- *Canada Millennium Scholarship Foundation.* In its 1998 budget, the federal Department of Finance announced that, beginning in 2000, the government will hand out scholarships to 100,000 students, averaging $3,000 per student per year, up to a maximum of $15,000 per student over four years. Free money from the government! Not a bad deal. These scholarships will be awarded to students attending virtually any postsecondary educational institution, including colleges, universities, CEGEPs (Québec's *Colleges d'enseignement général et professionel*), vocational and technical institutes, and foreign schools.

Action Step

You'll find a terrific resource for locating free money online at the Web site www.studentawards.com. At this site you'll need to register online and complete a questionnaire, providing details about your child, but your child can expect to qualify for approximately 20 different awards if he's like most students. In fact, if your child qualifies for fewer than 10 awards, you should tinker with your responses to the questionnaire slightly to include more interests and so on. You and your child are responsible for applying for the awards, but this Web site will set you in the right direction.

How does the government propose to pay for this free money? In 1998 a foundation was set up and funded with $2.5 billion from the federal coffers.

By the way, these scholarships will be handed out on the basis of need to low- and middle-income students.

TO MAKE A LONG STORY SHORT:

- Thousands of scholarships, awards, bursaries, and grants are available.

- Begin by asking high school guidance counsellors, employers, and various colleges and universities if they have, or know of, any free money available.

- Don't forget about funds that may be available from a variety of sources, earmarked for certain types of students.

Tim's Tip 13: Contact the federal and provincial governments for more information about free money available from them.

Wondering whom you should contact at the federal and provincial levels to talk about free money? Here's a list of addresses and phone numbers, current at the time of writing:

Federal Government

The Learning and Literacy Directorate
Human Resources Development Canada
P.O. Box 2090, Station D
Ottawa ON K1P 6C6
Phone: (819) 994-1844
Toll-free: 1-888-432-7377 (English); 1-800-733-3765 (French)
TTY: (819) 994-1218
Internet: www.hrdc-drhc.gc.ca/student_loans

Provinces and Territories

Newfoundland

Student Aid Division
Department of Education
P.O. Box 8700
St. John's NF A1B 4J6
Phone: (709) 729-4244
Toll-free: 1-888-657-0800
Fax: (709) 729-2298
Internet: www.edu.gov.nf.ca/studentaid/

Prince Edward Island

Student Financial Services
Department of Education
P.O. Box 2000
105 Rochford St.
Shaw Building, 3rd Floor
Charlottetown PE C1A 7N8
Phone: (902) 368-4640
Fax: (902) 368-6144
Internet: www.gov.pe.ca/educ/resources/stu_aid/index.asp

Nova Scotia

Student Assistance Office
Department of Education and Culture
P.O. Box 2290, Halifax Central
Halifax NS B3J 3C8
Phone: (902) 424-8420
Toll-free: 1-800-565-8420 (within Nova Scotia)
TDD: (902) 424-2058
Fax: (902) 424-0540
Internet: www.ednet.ns.ca/educ/student/index.html

New Brunswick
Student Services Branch
Department of Education
P.O. Box 6000, 548 York Street
Fredericton NB E3B 5H1
Phone: (506) 453-2577
Toll-free: 1-800-667-5626 (within Atlantic Provinces, Québec,
and Ontario)
Fax: (506) 444-4333
Internet: www.gov.nb.ca/ael/stuaid/e/guide.htm

Québec
Aide financière aux études
Ministère de l'Éducation
1035, rue De La Chevrotière
Québec QC G1R 5A5
Phone: 1-888-345-4505 (outside Québec)
(418) 646-4505 (Québec)
(514) 864-4505 (Montréal)
Internet: www.meq.gouv.qc.ca/afe/index.html

Ontario
Student Support Branch
Ministry of Training, Colleges and Universities
P.O. Box 4500
189 Red River Road, 4th Floor
Thunder Bay ON P7B 6G9
Phone: (807) 343-7260
Toll-free: 1-800-465-3013 (Ontario only)
TDD: 1-800-465-3958 (Ontario only)
Fax: (807) 343-7278
Internet: osap.gov.on.ca

Manitoba

Student Financial Assistance

Manitoba Education and Training

409–1181 Portage Avenue

Winnipeg MB R3G 0T3

Phone: (204) 945-6321 (in Manitoba)

(204) 945-2313 (out of province)

Toll-free: 1-800-204-1685 (in Manitoba)

Fax: (204) 948-3421

Internet: www.edu.gov.mb.ca/postsec/finance/finance.html

Saskatchewan

Student Financial Assistance Unit

Saskatchewan Post-secondary Education and Skills Training

Room B21, Walter Scott Building, Albert Street

Regina SK S4P 3V7

Phone: (306) 787-5620

Toll-free: 1-800-597-8278 (except in Ontario)

Fax: (306)787-7537

Internet: www.sasked.gov.sk.ca/P/departmental/index.html

Alberta

Alberta Students Finance

Alberta Advanced Education and Career Development

(Information and counselling services related to student funding are
available at all Alberta Career Development Centres. Please consult the
telephone directory or visit www.alis.gov.ab.ca/learning/Financial.htm
for the centre nearest you.)

Internet: www.alis.gov.ab.ca/learning/finance.html

British Columbia

Student Services Branch

Ministry of Advanced Education, Training and Technology

P.O. Box 9173

Station Provincial Government

Victoria BC V8W 9H7

Phone: (250) 387-6100 (Victoria only)

(250) 660-2610 (Lower Mainland only)

Toll-free: 1-800-561-1818 (in British Columbia)

Fax: (250) 356-9455

Internet: www.aett.gov.bc.ca/studentservices

Yukon

Students Financial Assistance Unit

Advanced Education Branch

Department of Education

P.O. Box 2703

Whitehorse YK Y1A 2C6

Phone: (867) 667-5929

Toll-free: 1-800-661-0408 (Yukon only)

Fax: (867) 667-8555

Internet: www.yesnet.yk.ca/sites/sfa

Northwest Territories

Student Financial Assistance

Department of Education, Culture and Employment

P.O. Box 1320

Yellowknife NT X1A 2L9

Phone: (867) 873-7190

Toll-free: 1-800-661-0793

Fax: (867) 873-0336

Toll-free fax: 1-800-661-0893

Internet: siksik.learnnet.nt.ca/income/html/sfamain.htm

Nunavut

Canada's newest territory has not yet set up student assistance
services. Students are referred to the Northwest Territories (see above).

This information can be obtained in alternative formats by contacting the federal government's InfoTouch service. Call 1-800-788-8282 on your touch-tone phone or through your TTY device (teletypewriter). The documents you request are automatically produced in the format selected and mailed directly to you. If you have Internet access, visit the above-listed Web sites that are appropriate for your situation. You might find that all your questions are answered there.

What's that? You're not convinced that our governments are giving away free money? Think again. The Canada Student Loans Program provides more than just loans to students. Your child may be eligible for free money—in some cases, Canada Study Grants (CSGs). For example:

- *Students with disabilities* may be eligible for up to $5,000 in grants to assist in paying for equipment or services they need to attend school.

- *High-need part-time students* who can demonstrate their financial need may qualify for a grant of up to $1,200.

- *Students with dependants* who can demonstrate a financial need of more than $275 per week in combined federal and provincial loans may be eligible for grants of up to $40 per week, if they have one

Did You Know?

The government provides all the information you'll ever need about Canada Study Grants in a booklet called *Canada Student Loans Program, Full-time and Part-time Students Information Guide*. If you're looking for a copy you can contact Human Resources Development Canada through the blue pages in your phone book. Make sure you ask for publication number Y-232-07-98. And tell them Tim sent you— you'll get the booklet for free. All right, I confess, the booklet's free anyway.

or two dependants, or up to $60 per week, if they have three or more dependants.

- *Women pursuing a PhD* may be entitled to grants of up to $9,000 over a three-year period if they are studying in fields typically dominated by men, including engineering, applied sciences, mathematics, physical sciences, and certain other fields where the participation rate for women is 35 percent or less.

One last point: Your province may be willing to chip in some more free money if you qualify. It can't hurt to ask.

TO MAKE A LONG STORY SHORT:

- Be sure to call the federal and your provincial government to enquire about free money.

- Visit the appropriate Web sites listed above. You might find all the information you're looking for.

Tim's Tip 14: Don't forget to set aside funds to cover the tax bill on your free money.

I've always thought the kid next door was a little weird. Jeremy is 18 years old now, heading to university for the first time. He's got glasses thick enough to double as paperweights, and his favourite pastime seems to be studying logarithms. I've always thought he's the type of kid who would study something requiring very little interaction with people. We had a good talk recently, and I asked what he was going to study in university.

"Accounting and tax," he told me. (Turns out Jeremy's not such a weird kid after all.) "I'm going to win the Nobel prize for accounting."

"I didn't know there was such a thing," I said. "But if you happen to win, it'll be tax-free since it's considered to be a 'prescribed' prize."

Jeremy was fascinated. Let me explain the taxation of free money.

Scholarships, Awards, Bursaries, Grants, and Fellowships

If a student receives any of these awards, it's taxable under paragraph 56(1)(n) of the federal *Income Tax Act*. The good news? The first $500 is excluded from income. Further, if the student uses the financial assistance in the production of a literary, dramatic, musical, or artistic work, the tax-free portion can be as high as the total of all costs that were incurred to meet the conditions of the financial assistance. These costs could include travel, meals, and lodging expenses, but not expenses that were reimbursed or are otherwise deductible. In addition, certain "prescribed" prizes are not taxable. These are prizes that are awarded in recognition of certain achievements, but not for services rendered.

Research Grants (Stipends)

Sorry, but research grants are taxable. Paragraph 56(1)(o) of the *Income Tax Act* says so. Students may deduct from these grants any expenses incurred in performing the research work, including travel, meals, and lodging, but not including expenses that were reimbursed

---

STUDENT TAX ESTIMATOR

Student's Taxable Income
(Including Scolarships, Bursaries, etc.) —————— A

Deduct:

Basic amount	7,131
First $500 of scholarships, awards, bursaries, grants, fellowships	————
Tuition fees	————
$200 times number of months in full-time enrollment in school	————
$60 times number of months in part-time enrollment in school	————

Total deductions —————— B

Income subject to tax (A-B) —————— C

Tax at 26% (C X 26%) ══════

Note: This estimator assumes the student's taxable income is less than $29,590 and that the student is not entitled to non-refundable credits other than the basic personal amount and tuition and education credits.

or are otherwise deductible. As a rule of thumb, a student can estimate the amount of tax owing in a year by using the table on page 46.

A student's best bet is to plan for these taxes ahead of time by setting money aside as she earns it. This way, there won't be any ugly surprises at tax time. Exams are enough of a burden in April.

TO MAKE A LONG STORY SHORT:

- Free money is usually taxable, except for the first $500 received.

- Estimate the taxes owing for the year, and if you expect a tax balance owing, have your child plan to set aside money as it's earned to cover the tax bill that will be due in April.

Borrowing For Education

In addition to begging for free money, your child can borrow to cover the cost of a postsecondary education. The fact is, borrowing to acquire an education has become a national pastime of sorts. And it's understandable. With the cost of education rising, it's not easy finding the resources to pay for an education without borrowing.

In June 1997, Statistics Canada, in conjunction with Human Resources Development Canada, conducted a National Graduates Survey, interviewing nearly 43,000 people who had graduated from college or university in 1995. The former students who were surveyed most frequently identified, as their primary source of education funds, employment earnings (59 percent of college graduates and 69 percent of those with a bachelor's degree) and student loan programs (41 percent of college grads and 42 percent of those with a bachelor's degree). In third place? Mom and dad ranked close behind student loans.

In total, the study showed that 46 percent of college graduates and 50 percent of those with bachelor's degrees had borrowed from a student loan program.

Tim's Tip 15: Shake the trend that has students borrowing more than ever while making repayments at a slower pace.

Compared to the class of 1982, 1995 graduates owed between 130 percent and 140 percent more to student loan programs (after adjusting for inflation) at graduation, according to Statistics Canada.

Did You Know?

Graduates in 1995 owed, on average, $9,600 (college grads) and $13,300 (those with a bachelor's degree) when they graduated. But there's more. A full 22 percent of those with a bachelor's degree owed more than $20,000 at graduation (the figure is 7 percent for college students). And get this: Statistics Canada has calculated that the average debt load at graduation in 1998 for those with a bachelor's degree was $25,000! That's right, a big jump from $13,300 just three years before.

Not only have students been borrowing more, they have been repaying their loans more slowly. Of those who graduated in 1995, 17 percent of those who had borrowed for college and 23 percent of those who had borrowed for a bachelor's degree were not making loan payments on their education debt two years after graduation. In fact, many of those students (11 percent of college graduates and 16 percent of bachelor's degree graduates) actually owed more two years after graduation than they did on graduation day. In total, 1995 college graduates paid off just 19 percent of their loans within two years of graduation, while 1990 graduates paid off 35 percent of their loans within the same period. For bachelor's degree holders, the percentages are 17 percent and 27 percent respectively.

Shaking the Trend

There are two key problems with borrowing more for education (that is, relying less on other funding sources) and paying off the debt more slowly than absolutely necessary.

First, there's the cost of borrowing. Loans don't come free. Your child is going to have to pay interest on any borrowed money. Consider the cost of borrowing $25,000 for an education. If the loan is repaid over 10 years and we assume an interest rate of 9.5 percent, the total interest costs alone will be $13,819. That's right, your child's total loan payments will be over 55 percent higher than the $25,000 borrowed.

Second, there's the impact on credit records and other borrowing capacity. If your child fails to make good on the required student loan payments, her credit record will show this. Further, the fact that your child has this education debt will by itself change her chances of borrowing for other important reasons—to buy a home or car or to invest in a business. In short, a bad credit record or an unpaid education loan could reduce your child's likelihood of borrowing for other reasons.

How can a student avoid the tendency to borrow more than necessary? How can she avoid stretching the loan payments out longer than makes sense? It's not rocket science, but here's the plan:

- *Take full advantage of any free money before applying for loans.* It's surprising how few students take the time to look for free money.

- *Work hard and save hard during summer months.* The summer months provide students with an opportunity to make enough money to significantly contribute to their education costs.

- *Work part-time during the school year.* While this is a legitimate—and possibly necessary—strategy, I don't believe students should work more than 15 hours each week. I'll come back to this concept in Tip 25.

- *Maximize earnings after graduation.* This point may seem a little obvious, but low income is the number one reason for taking too long to pay off student debt. Of those with incomes below $30,000 who graduated in 1995, nearly three times as many had trouble paying off their student loans as graduates with incomes over $50,000. If your child is going to borrow for education, she should consider a field of study that will make it easier to find a job after graduation. Check out these statistics on student debt by field of study:

- *Consider delaying additional education.* Of those who graduated in 1995, 31 percent of college and 45 percent of bachelor's degree graduates were back in school within two years after their first graduation. Further education might be just what your child needs, but careful thought should be given to when it should take place. For a student who is knee-deep in debt, it might make sense to delay the final leg of education until sources of funding other than debt can be found.

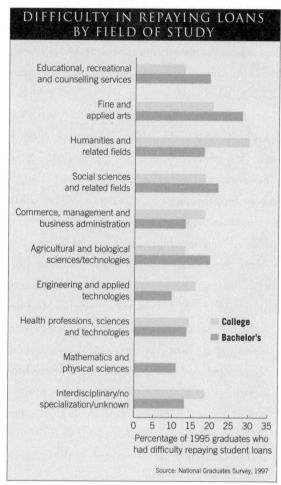

DIFFICULTY IN REPAYING LOANS BY FIELD OF STUDY

Educational, recreational and counselling services

Fine and applied arts

Humanities and related fields

Social sciences and related fields

Commerce, management and business administration

Agricultural and biological sciences/technologies

Engineering and applied technologies

Health professions, sciences and technologies

Mathematics and physical sciences

Interdisciplinary/no specialization/unknown

College
Bachelor's

0 5 10 15 20 25 30 35
Percentage of 1995 graduates who had difficulty repaying student loans

Source: National Graduates Survey, 1997

TO MAKE A LONG STORY SHORT:

- Student debt loads have been rising steadily. The average student faced $25,000 of debt at graduation in 1998, up from $13,300 just three years before.

- Students are paying off their education debt more slowly than ever before.

- The result of significant unpaid student debt may be an ugly credit rating and an inability to borrow for important things.

- Your child should take steps to shake the trend towards higher student debt, which is being paid off more slowly than ever before.

Tim's Tip 16: **Look first to the Canada Student Loans Program when borrowing money.**

Despite the high cost of borrowing, over half of all students this year will need some kind of loan assistance to pay for school. In 1997–98, Ottawa lent out $1.62 billion to approximately 350,000 students (362,490 loans). These loans are administered under the Canada Student Loans Program (CSLP). Loans are available for both full-time and part-time study, as long as the student meets the criteria.

Who Is Eligible for the CSLP?

Good question. If your child hopes to receive a loan under the CSLP, he has to meet the following criteria:

- be a Canadian citizen or permanent resident;
- reside in a province that participates in the CSLP (Québec and the Northwest Territories have their own programs to which the feds contribute, so students in these jurisdictions would not apply under the CSLP);
- demonstrate to the provincial student assistance office that his resources are not enough to cover the costs of education;
- enroll in at least 60 percent (40 percent for a disabled student) of a full-time course load at a designated postsecondary educational institution; part-time students should enroll in between 20 percent and 59 percent of a full-time course load (between 20 percent and 39 percent for disabled part-time students;

- enroll, or qualify to enroll, in a program leading to a degree, diploma, or certificate (of at least 12 weeks in length within a period of 15 consecutive weeks); and
- have a gross family income under certain thresholds.

How Much Can My Child Borrow?

Your child will be able to borrow an amount that varies on the basis of financial need. In particular, he will be able to borrow 60 percent of his "assessed need," to a maximum of $165 per week of full-time study. A full-time student can collect for up to 340 weeks of study (400 weeks for PhD students, and 520 weeks for students with disabilities).

Just to set the record straight, here is the actual calculation for a student loan under this program: assessed costs – assessed resources = assessed need.

Your child's assessed costs are the costs you would expect to

Make a calculation to estimate the loan your child is likely to receive from the federal government. Just visit the following Web site (it has a calculator you can use to estimate the loan): *www.hrdc-drhc.gc.ca/ student_loans/ engraph/ snas.html.*
Keep two things in mind: This calculation doesn't include loans that might be available from your provincial government, and the federal government will fund just 60 percent of your child's assessed need—max. So you'll want to approach the province in which you live for additional funding, if it's required. (See the list of provincial sources under Tip 13.)

associate with education, including tuition, books and supplies, a living allowance, and transportation. The assessed resources part of the equation includes a portion (about 53 percent) of the income your child expects to earn in the summer and during the school year, the value of certain assets your child may own (RRSPs, vehicles, and other financial assets), and contributions that you as a parent are expected to make. Here's the deal: Even if you don't plan to contribute financially to your child's education, his loan under the CSLP will still be affected by your income. The excess of your child's assessed costs over his assessed resources equals his assessed need.

When Will My Child Have to Repay the Loan?

Yes, your child will have to pay the piper at some point. The rules say that your child has to begin making loan payments six months after graduation. How does this work? At the end of your child's study period, he should visit his lender and complete a Consolidated Student Loan Agreement, which will provide for repayment to begin after the six-month window is past. Interest on the loan during the time your child is in school is paid by the federal government. Your child is responsible for paying interest on the outstanding loan from the date of graduation, even though payments are not required until six months after graduation.

Where Does My Child Apply?

All it takes is a visit to your child's educational institution or the provincial or territorial student assistance office closest to your home. Again, check out the list of provincial offices under Tip 13.

TO MAKE A LONG STORY SHORT:

- When borrowing money, look first to the Canada Student Loans Program. Visit your child's school or the appropriate provincial student assistance office to apply.

- The amount of the loan will depend on your child's assessed need, which simply equals the expected costs of his education less the resources available to pay for those costs.

- A full-time student can borrow up to 60 percent of his assessed need, to a maximum of $165 per week of schooling.

- Repayments must begin six months after graduation.

Tim's Tip 17: **Look to your bank for a loan if your child doesn't qualify for the CSLP.**

A few of the big banks will offer students a line of credit as a form of loan for the purposes of attending school. Normally your child would pursue such a line of credit if she doesn't qualify for a loan under the CSLP. The Royal Bank, Bank of Nova Scotia, and Bank of Montreal all offer lines of credit that allow students to borrow up to $5,000 each year ($10,000 annually for graduate students), up to a maximum of $30,000. The big difference between a line of credit and a CSLP loan is that you can't count on the government to pick up the tab for any of the interest on the loan. Your child is on the hook for all the interest, from day one.

Don't be surprised if the bank wants a co-signer for the line of credit (guess who that's likely to be?) and a budget detailing how your child intends to manage her money. Accessing the line of credit can be as simple for your child as using a bank card or credit card.

TO MAKE A LONG STORY SHORT:

- When a CSLP loan is not an option, a personal line of credit may be available to your child through a bank.

- Advances of $5,000 each year ($10,000 for graduate students) may be available, to a total maximum of $30,000.

- The interest costs are borne by your child, not the federal government, and your child may need a co-signer for the line of credit.

Tim's Tip 18: **Be sure to claim tax and other relief for interest paid on student loans.**

The 1998 federal budget was kind to students who financed, or who plan to finance, their education with loans. In that budget, the Department of Finance announced two key changes to the treatment of interest on student loans: a tax credit available for interest paid on student loans, and improved interest relief for up to 30 months. The name of the game here is to take advantage of all the relief possible.

Tax Credit for Interest Costs

Beginning with the 1998 tax year, the tax collector has allowed students to claim a federal tax credit equal to 17 percent of all interest paid in the year on a student loan. After factoring in the effect of this credit on provincial income taxes, the total tax savings to students should amount to approximately 26 percent of the interest paid each year. If your child doesn't have enough income to make use of the credit to bring his taxes down to nil, the credit can be carried forward for up to five years and used in those subsequent years. See Tip 61 for more.

Most students don't need the tax credit available on their student loan interest to reduce their tax liability to nil during the years they're in school. While this tax credit can be carried forward to be used in a future year, it will expire if not used after five years. To avoid expiry, instruct your child to hold off on claiming RRSP deductions after graduation until the tax credits for loan interest have been used up. Don't get me wrong. RRSP contributions should be made, but the deduction can be held back until after the loan interest credits are used.

*L*et's move the clock forward 17 years to when Chloe will be age 22. Assume that Chloe borrows $30,000 over four years of university, which she will pay back over 10 years, making *monthly payments of $390 on the loan (a total of $4,680 for the year 2018). Her total interest costs in 2018 will amount to $2,545. Her tax credit in 2018 will amount to 17 percent of $2,545, or $433 federally. The federal and provincial tax savings combined will equal approximately $662. Over the course of the 10-year loan, her total tax savings will amount to approximately $4,310.*

Improved Interest Relief

If your child is having a tough time repaying a student loan, the government's Interest Relief Plan (IRP) could help out. Under the IRP, the federal government may pay the interest on your child's student loan for a three-month period, which can be extended to a maximum of 30 months over the life of the loan. Your child can apply for the IRP by getting the forms from the lending institution that holds his loan, from Human Resources Development Canada, or from your provincial or territorial student assistance office.

Not everyone qualifies for the IRP. Your family's income has to be low enough to warrant this help. (The threshold varies based on the size of your family and the magnitude of the monthly loan payment.) In certain special circumstances—for example, if unexpected emergency expenses arise—your child might qualify for the IRP.

In addition to the income requirements to qualify, the following conditions must also be met to take advantage of the IRP:

- The student must live in Canada or be on a government-sponsored international internship.
- The student must have signed a Consolidated Student Loan Agreement.
- The student must not have already received interest relief for the maximum 30 months allowed.
- The student must not have defaulted on any Canada Student Loan for which the government has already reimbursed the lender.

I should mention here that after your child has taken advantage of the IRP for 30 months, he may take advantage of an option to extend the repayment period of the student loan to as long as 15 years, or request a reduction in the loan principal. I'll talk more about these options under Tip 19.

TO MAKE A LONG STORY SHORT:

- Relief for student interest comes in two forms: a tax credit for interest paid; and, if your family is experiencing financial hardship, assistance from the government, under the Interest Relief Plan, to cover interest costs for up to 30 months.

- Take advantage of all relief available to reduce the burden of interest costs.

Tim's Tip 19: **Don't declare bankruptcy to avoid student debt—better options are available.**

Let's face it, with student debt on the rise, the likelihood that more students will declare bankruptcy because of an inability to pay off their debt will probably also rise. I'll tell you up front, I'm not a big fan of bankruptcy as a way of dealing with student debt. In fact, I think that in most cases it's pretty irresponsible to take this measure, for two reasons.

First, any student who declares bankruptcy is shooting herself in the foot—which can hurt. You see, after declaring bankruptcy, the student is obligated to inform not only all potential creditors of her status as an undischarged bankrupt, but all those with whom she has business dealings of any type. As you might guess, this situation will make it tough to get back on track financially.

Second, declaring bankruptcy leaves the rest of us holding the bag for the student's debt, since the government uses taxpayers' money to pay a "risk premium" to the lending banks as insurance on uncollectible loans.

In 1997–98, the federal government paid $58.5 million in risk premiums to lending institutions. This premium can only increase if the instances of bankruptcy rise.

Take a look at the chart below on increased student bankruptcies.

CANADA STUDENT LOAN PROGRAM BANKRUPTCY CLAIMS	
Year	Recipients declaring bankruptcy
1990–91	3,300
1991–92	4,500
1992–93	4,500
1993–94	7,800
1994–95	7,000
1995–96	7,850
1996–97	11,800
Source: Human Resources Development Canada	

New Rules About Student Bankruptcy

For the most part, student loan debts are treated exactly the same as all other unsecured debts, in that creditors are prevented from taking collection action during a bankruptcy, but they will get their share of any distributions, and they have the same rights as creditors in other bankruptcies.

But the rules have changed for people with outstanding student loans who declare bankruptcy, because of amendments made to the *Banking and Insolvency Act* in June 1998. Formerly, a person who filed for bankruptcy within two years of last attending school would be ineligible to have her student loans discharged at the end of the nine-month bankruptcy term. She'd have to wait until that two-year period was over. Now, a person who files for bankruptcy within 10 (not 2) years of last attending school can only apply to have her student loans discharged at the end of the 10-year period. Ten years is a long time to be considered an undischarged bankrupt. Remember, an undischarged bankrupt is required to tell all potential creditors and those with whom she has business dealings that she is an undischarged bankrupt—and it's not a nice label to wear.

Better Options

If your child finds herself unable to make good on her student loans, she has options that, to my mind, are more attractive than bankruptcy.

- *Make a consumer proposal.* It's possible to make a consumer proposal to your creditors, based on your circumstances. For example, you can ask the creditors to reduce the amounts owing to them or request more time to pay the amounts due. The rules require that a consumer proposal be made to all preferred and unsecured creditors, but it doesn't usually affect the rights of secured creditors. The terms of the proposal must be completed in five years and must offer the creditors at least what they would be paid in a bankruptcy. Some student loan authorities have accepted consumer proposals and have even agreed to forgive the balance owing on completion of the proposal.

- *Extend repayment of the loan.* I mentioned in Tip 18 that it's possible to ask for interest relief if your child and family are experiencing financial difficulties. In this case, the government will pick up the tab for the interest on the student loan for a period of up to 30 months. If, after this 30-month period, your child is still unable to meet her loan payments, she can ask the financial institution to extend the loan repayment to 15 years. Such an arrangement would lower the monthly payments by almost 25 percent at current interest rates.

- Ask for debt reduction. What happens if extending the loan repayment period just doesn't provide enough help?

Caution!

Too many young people look at bankruptcy as the easy way out, not fully understanding the implications. To avoid the potential for bankruptcy, explain to your child that her total debt payments each year should not exceed 40 percent of her gross income. I'm talking about all debt payments: student loans, credit cards, car loans, lines of credit, you name it. For example, if her annual salary is $40,000, she's heading for problems if her total debt payments exceed $16,000 (40 percent of $40,000) annually.

The federal government will reduce your child's loan principal if the annual payments exceed a given percentage of her income. The maximum debt reduction is $10,000 or 50 percent of the loan principal, whichever is less. To qualify for this reduction, five years must have passed since your child finished school, and the interest relief option (discussed under Tip 18) must have been exhausted.

By the way, if your child insists on the bankruptcy option, she should visit a trustee in bankruptcy. Many accountants and lawyers are licensed as trustees. A trustee can set the record straight about your child's rights and responsibilities in bankruptcy.

TO MAKE A LONG STORY SHORT:

- Bankruptcy is one way of dealing with student debt when the burden gets too high. New rules, however, may not allow the loan to be discharged until 10 years have passed since the person last attended school.

- Bankruptcy should be a last resort. Better options exist, including making a consumer proposal, extending the repayment period of the loan, asking for interest relief (discussed under Tip 18), and requesting a reduction in the loan principal.

Stealing For Education

In addition to begging and borrowing to get through school, your child has the option of stealing. Now, hold on. I'm not talking about a bank heist, fraud, embezzlement, or any other illegal act. (We wouldn't want your child graduating with a criminal record.) I'm simply referring to "stealing" from your own lifestyle and retirement assets or from your other cash resources in the years your child attends college or university.

Tim's Tip 20: **Use your lifestyle assets for education only as a last resort.**

Randy, Skye, and I were relaxing by the pool when we started chatting about Randy's hobby. He's a collector. What does he collect? Everything: city maps, pop bottles, hockey cards, string, comic books, business cards (he has over 13,000 now), autographs, and the usual stamps and coins. Skye, on the other hand, doesn't collect anything— except bug bites. The mosquitoes were not kind to Skye last summer.

"Tim, I figure all my collections are worth about $50,000 by now," Randy said.

"That's great, Randy. So what are you going to do with all that stuff?" I asked.

"Keep it," he replied.

Skye had other plans. "Randy, I think we should sell it and buy something exotic that we can't afford to buy otherwise."

"How about an education for Chloe and Joshua?" I offered. From the look on Skye's face, I don't think that's what she had in mind.

"Hold on!" Randy said. "These things are my pride and joy. I don't want to part with them—even for the kids' education—if I don't have to."

Randy hit the nail on the head. It's always an option to sell some of your "lifestyle assets" to pay for your child's education, but do you really want to part with that time-share unit, motorcycle, cottage, boat, antique collection, autographed Wayne Gretzky poster, or 1972 Philips electronic toothbrush? Fat chance. Of course your child's education is ultimately more important than these things, but holding onto them may be important for sentimental reasons.

J*anet recognizes that helping to put Allison through school, starting in just three years, is going to be tough. In addition to looking for free money and student loans, Janet plans to sell a number of items that she inherited from her grandmother and that have been appraised at about $20,000. While she would choose to keep the antiques if she could, Allison's education is more important. Selling them means that Allison is able to borrow $20,000 less to get her through school. Considering the interest costs that would have accumulated on $20,000, if she had borrowed it, her mother's gesture will save Allison about $31,000 in total payments after she graduates. It's doubtful that those antiques would have appreciated in value to $31,000 over the same term as the likely term of a student loan, so the investment decision is not a bad one for Janet and Allison.*

TO MAKE A LONG STORY SHORT:

• Lifestyle assets include items such as a cottage, boat, collections, furniture, and the like. Selling some of these to free up cash to help pay for the education of your child can make sense, but it should be a last-resort maneuver.

Tim's Tip 21: Avoid dipping into your retirement assets at all costs.

While it's important that your child get an education, it's even more important that you have the financial resources to survive for your lifetime. Your retirement income comes first, your child's education second. You should therefore avoid dipping into your registered retirement savings plan (RRSP) or other retirement nest egg to pay for your child's education.

You may have heard about the new tax measures that were introduced in the 1998 federal budget that allow Canadians to access their RRSPs for education under the Life Long Learning Plan (LLLP). That plan, which I'll discuss more in Chapter 6, is only available to you if you withdraw funds for your own or your spouse's education, not for your kids' education. I'm not condemning withdrawals under that plan.

You could be heading for disaster if you haven't taken the time to figure out how much money you'll need in retirement and whether you're on the right track to getting there. Before using any of your retirement assets for your child's education— and it's a decision that should be a last resort—be sure to determine whether you've set aside enough for your retirement. A good financial adviser can help you to make this determination if you're not sure how to do it yourself. As a guideline, a person who is 45 years old today and wants to retire at age 65 and live to 85 with the equivalent of $50,000 of income annually had better have $1,230,000 set aside by age 65.

Caution!

In this tip, I'm referring to the concept of making taxable withdrawals from your RRSP to provide cash to pay for your child's education. In most cases, this is a very bad idea. As I said, your retirement comes first. Not only will you hurt the growth of your retirement nest egg by making withdrawals, but you'll lose that valuable RRSP contribution room forever. What I mean is, if you were to withdraw, say, $10,000 from your RRSP, Revenue Canada would not restore to you the $10,000 of contribution room that you used up when you put that $10,000 into the RRSP in the first place. No way. That room is gone for good.

I would make one exception to the general rule that you

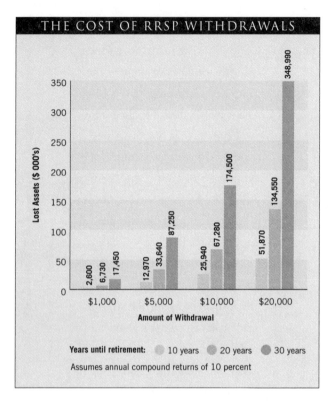

THE COST OF RRSP WITHDRAWALS

Lost Assets ($ 000's)

350
300
250
200
150
100
50
0

$1,000 $5,000 $10,000 $20,000

Amount of Withdrawal

2,600
6,730
17,450
12,970
33,640
87,250
25,940
67,280
174,500
51,870
134,550
348,990

Years until retirement: 10 years   20 years   30 years

Assumes annual compound returns of 10 percent

shouldn't withdraw money from your RRSP to fund your child's education. If you have taken the time to calculate how much you'll need in your RRSP at retirement, and you have much more than you need (a rare situation indeed), then and only then should you consider making withdrawals to pay for a child's education.

To give you some idea of how RRSP withdrawals for your child's education (or for any reason) can hurt you, consider the numbers above.

TO MAKE A LONG STORY SHORT:

- While your child's education is important, your retirement nest egg comes first. Don't make withdrawals from your RRSP or other retirement savings for your child's education if at all possible.

- The only exception to this rule would be if you have more than you need set aside for retirement, which is a rare occurrence.

- I'm not referring here to the Life Long Learning Plan, which allows you to make withdrawals from an RRSP for your education or that of your spouse, but not your child's. I'll talk more about this plan in Chapter 6.

Tim's Tip 22: **Plan to use some of your other cash resources for your child's education.**

In addition to stealing from your lifestyle and retirement assets, which I generally discourage, you may be able to help finance your child's education by stealing from your other cash resources. Three resources may apply here:

* your disposable income in the years your child is in school
* lines of credit
* non-retirement investments (which can include mutual funds, stocks, bonds, cash deposits, insurance policies, and more)

It's only prudent to think ahead of time about how much you'll have available to contribute from these sources. In my experience, most people are able to contribute relatively little from their disposable income because that income is already spoken for. If, however, you can make a contribution from your disposable income, then part of your education savings strategy might include such a contribution.

Using a line of credit to finance a child's education will certainly help your child, and can make sense as long as incurring this debt doesn't jeopardize your retirement savings and you will have the cash flow in the future to pay off the debt.

Your non-retirement investments can be used in two ways to provide for your child's education. First, the assets can be liquidated to provide cash for your child to attend school. Alternatively, the assets might provide a stream of income for this purpose. Selling the investments may incur a tax cost if the investments have appreciated in value, so make sure you calculate this tax bill first. As for using the income earned on the investments for education purposes, focus on generating dividend rather than interest income, since the income will be taxable in your hands. Dividends from Canadian corporations are taxed very efficiently—a maximum tax rate of approximately 33 percent, compared to the highest rate on interest income (which varies by province) of approximately 50 percent. (You'll find complete tables of marginal tax rates in my book *Winning the Tax Game*.)

If you decide to use any of these other cash resources to partially fund your child's education, keep in mind that your retirement savings come first. If you will jeopardize your retirement savings by using these other resources, don't do it!

TO MAKE A LONG STORY SHORT:

• Plan on using some of your other cash resources for your child's education. These resources include disposable income, a line of credit, and non-retirement investment assets.

• Whatever you do, don't jeopardize your retirement savings by using these other resources.

Stealing from your lifestyle assets should only be done as a last resort, and stealing from your retirement assets is not an option except in rare situations. Plan to use some of your other cash resources to contribute to your child's education, provided you don't jeopardize your retirement savings. Keep these rules of thumb in mind as you plan to meet the education costs of your kids.

Sweating For Education

In addition to begging, borrowing, and stealing, your child can sweat his way through college or university. Tell him this is called the "earning while you're learning" plan. I'm talking here about your child working full-time during the months when he is not in school, and part-time while attending school. Most students work full-time in the summer (or other months when not in school), and some also work part-time when in full-time attendance at a college or university.

Tim's Tip 23: **Encourage your child to use employment as a means of raising money and gaining valuable experience.**

There's no doubt that an education is important, but there's nothing like real-world experience to teach your child the ins and outs of a particular job or field of study. Your child should look at one of two options to make sure he is gaining the kind of experience that is important—a cooperative study program or a targeted employment search.

Cooperative Study Program

More and more colleges and universities are offering co-op programs that provide career-related job experience. The requirements for participating in a co-op program can vary. Some programs are designed for senior students, while others are open to students in their first year.

It's common, for example, for students studying accounting (and what could be more exciting?) to study for four months, work for four months in an accounting firm, and then repeat this cycle until all courses are complete. It's usually true that students in a co-op program take slightly longer to graduate because of the intervening work terms. Most of the time, however, students in a co-op program graduate with a job—often with one of the employers who provided work throughout the years of schooling.

The real benefits of a co-op program are as follows:

- Funding for school is made easier by regular paid work terms.
- The program provides students with an opportunity to evaluate different jobs, so that they know ahead of time whether the field of study chosen is one they will really enjoy.
- Participation in the program often leads to a full-time job after graduation.

Targeted Employment Search

Perhaps your child's field of study doesn't offer a co-op program, or perhaps your child isn't interested in a co-op program and simply prefers to work during the summer months, and possibly during the school year as well. In this case, a targeted employment search makes a lot of sense.

A targeted employment search involves your child preparing a résumé, sending copies to a very specific ("targeted") list of potential employers, and following up those résumés with phone calls. Who should get a résumé? Your child should give some thought to the career field he would like to pursue. Any employers related to that field are good candidates, provided the commute from where your child lives to the employer is reasonable (unless your child is willing to relocate). If your child is not sure which career field to pursue, this strategy will provide an opportunity to try a particular career on for size.

Your child's résumé should be sent six to nine months in advance of when he hopes to work for an employer. Some students are guilty of waiting until school's out to start looking for a job. By the time exams are over, it's too late to find the best jobs—they were handed out in the previous fall or early in the new year. A telephone call from your child to each of the résumé recipients approximately three weeks after he has sent out the résumés will significantly improve his chances of finding a good job. In fact, according to Statistics Canada, contacting an employer may be the most effective means of finding a job.

Keep in mind: We're talking about employment with an objective. The objective is not only for your child to earn income to attend school, but to evaluate what type of job he would like after graduation. Encourage your child not to waste the opportunity to use work as a learning tool.

TO MAKE A LONG STORY SHORT:

- Working full-time between school terms and part-time while in full-time attendance at a college or university will not only provide income to help pay for education, but can provide your child with invaluable experience.

- One of two strategies should be utilized—a cooperative study program or a targeted employment search.

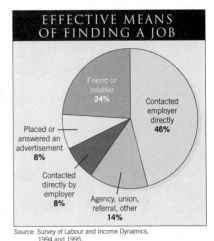

EFFECTIVE MEANS OF FINDING A JOB

Friend or relative 24%
Contacted employer directly 46%
Placed or answered an advertisement 8%
Contacted directly by employer 8%
Agency, union, referral, other 14%

Source: Survey of Labour and Income Dynamics, 1994 and 1995.

Tim's Tip 24: **Encourage your child to look for jobs on campus.**

If your child has decided to work during or between school terms, why not consider looking for a job right on campus? Most colleges and universities offer part-time jobs that are funded 100 percent by the school. Some jobs may be reserved for students who need financial aid but, for the most part, any student can apply for these jobs.

Many of these jobs (cashiers, food service workers, and the like) fall into the unskilled labour category, but other jobs (such as computer operator, or teaching or research assistant) provide a higher level of responsibility and usually a higher income. Some schools even provide temporary job services. These services work much like a temporary employment agency, but the jobs are usually on campus.

Suggest to your child that she visit the student employment or academic office on campus for a list of jobs available. Chances are good that the best jobs will disappear quickly, so she should start searching the first day of school, if not before.

TO MAKE A LONG STORY SHORT:

- Most colleges and universities offer a variety of jobs to students. Some require more skill than others and will pay more as a result.

- The best jobs will disappear quickly, so your child should start looking on the first day of school, if not before.

Tim's Tip 25: **Keep work time to a maximum of 15 hours a week, since education is the number one priority.**

If your child is going to enroll full-time at college or university, then he should treat his education as a full-time job. If he intends to work close to full-time hours, then he should really think about pursuing education on a part-time basis, which is a legitimate option in many programs.

It only makes sense that the more hours your child spends at work, the less time he will have for studying. This is true not only in university, but in high school as well. So, as your child approaches the end of his high school career—particularly the final two years where marks count the most in gaining acceptance to postsecondary school—make sure he has plenty of time to focus on studying and is not overburdened with work responsibilities. Although every child is different, you'll find that, on average, once your child is working more than 15 hours a week, his marks are likely to suffer.

TO MAKE A LONG STORY SHORT:

- If your child is enrolled full-time at college or university, he should treat it as a full-time job and work at employment on a part-time basis only.

- Even in your child's last two years of high school, he should not be burdened by excess work.

- Once your child works in excess of 15 hours a week, his marks are likely to be affected.

Saving For Education

In addition to begging, borrowing, stealing, and sweating to cover the costs of education, your family can save. This strategy is the most effective of all, provided you start early enough.

For Janet and her daughter, Allison, who is already 15, there have been no savings to date. Since Janet's income is relatively low, and she has just three years before Allison heads off to a postsecondary school, saving can't be their primary funding strategy.

By contrast, consider RJ and Lisa. They have three kids—Lindsay, age 15, Logan, age 12, and Jamie Ann, age 9. They live in the United States where they have been taking advantage of the American equivalent to Canada's registered education savings plan (RESP). They have already set enough aside for Lindsay, who will be going to college in three years, and if they maintain their monthly investment strategy, there will also be enough for Logan and Jamie Ann.

For the balance of the family (Skye and Randy, Judi and Ned, Janice and Peter, and Carolyn and me), our kids are very young and we still have time to put in place an effective savings strategy for their education.

One thing's for sure, whether you're starting late or have plenty of time to save, a savings program is important. Let's take a look at some of the basics.

If you invested $2,000 at the start of each year, beginning when your child is 1 year old, you could invest for 18 years. If we assume an 8 percent annual return on that money, you'd have $80,893 at the end of her 18th year. If you waited until your child was age 5 before starting to invest, $68,221 would be waiting there at the end of her 18th year. And if you waited until she was age 10 to start this program, you would have just $49,602 by the end of her 18th year. The moral of the story is obvious: Start early to maximize savings!

Tim's Tip 26: Start saving for your child's education as soon as possible, and save regularly.

This advice may seem like common sense, but saving for your child's education should begin today if you haven't already started. Time is your biggest ally when saving or investing. A few short years can make a big difference in how much money is accumulated.

Once you start a savings program, stick to it! Make it a regular habit, much like a mortgage payment. Arrange to have a pre-authorized payment deposited monthly into an investment account to make sure you're setting aside enough. Besides, it's much easier to budget when you're making regular monthly payments.

How Much Is Enough?

How much will you have to set aside to ensure there will be enough at the end of the day? It depends on how much time you have until your child goes to school, what percentage of the expected costs you hope to pay with the accumulated investments, and the after-tax rate of return on your investments.

The tables on the following page should give you a good idea of how much you need to save. The table you use will depend on whether you're expecting your child to live away from home or at home while attending college or university.

Let me explain how to use these tables. Suppose that your child is three years of age, and you want to save enough to allow her to live away from home. You would use the top table. Your child is likely to start postsecondary education in 2015, at which time four years of education is expected to cost $125,566 (if she lives away from home). If you can generate an annual return of 8 percent on your investments, then you would need to set aside $360 per month starting today to have enough in 2015 to cover 100 percent of your child's education costs.

LIVING AWAY FROM HOME					
Age of Child	First Year of Postsecondary Education	Expected Education Costs for Four Years	Monthly Investment Required Based on Expected Rate of Return		
			8%	10%	12%
Under 1	2018 $	149,709 $	310 $	247 $	195
1	2017	141,072	325	263	211
2	2016	133,040	341	280	229
3	2015	125,566	360	300	249
4	2014	118,606	383	323	272
5	2013	112,122	408	350	298
6	2012	106,077	438	381	329
7	2011	100,438	474	417	366
8	2010	95,173	517	461	410
9	2009	90,255	570	514	483
10	2008	85,857	636	581	530
11	2007	81,358	721	667	616
12	2006	77,326	855	782	731
13	2005	73,557	994	942	892
14	2004	70,019	1,234	1,183	1,132
15	2003	66,700	1,835	1,563	1,533

LIVING AT HOME					
Age of Child	First Year of Postsecondary Education	Expected Education Costs for Four Years	Monthly Investment Required Based on Expected Rate of Return		
			8%	10%	12%
Under 1	2018 $	112,295 $	232 $	185 $	147
1	2017	104,748	241	195	157
2	2016	97,774	251	206	166
3	2015	91,327	262	219	181
4	2014	85,365	275	233	196
5	2013	79,849	291	249	212
6	2012	74,744	309	265	292
7	2011	70,017	330	291	255
8	2010	65,638	356	318	283
9	2009	61,581	389	351	316
10	2008	57,816	429	392	358
11	2007	54,326	481	445	412
12	2006	51,086	551	516	483
13	2005	48,080	650	616	583
14	2004	45,284	798	765	732
15	2003	42,686	1,048	1,013	981

Now, suppose your child is eight years of age and you'd like to save enough for her to attend school while she is living at home. You would use the bottom table in this case. Your eight-year-old is expected to start college or university in 2010. By that time, you can expect four years of education to cost $65,638 (if she lives at home). If you expect to generate a 10 percent return on your money between now and then, you're going to have to set aside $318 monthly to have enough by the time she goes to school.

I'm sure you've got the hang of it now. But what if you don't plan to pay for 100 percent of your child's education costs through savings? In this case, simply pro-rate the monthly payment accordingly. For example, if you decide that you'd like to save 50 percent of the total education costs, with the balance paid for through begging, borrowing, stealing, or sweating, then take the monthly payment from the table and multiply it by 50 percent. If you want to save 75 percent of the expected costs with the balance coming from other sources, then calculate the monthly required savings as 75 percent of the payment amount in the table. Get the drift? Good.

TO MAKE A LONG STORY SHORT:

- Decide what percentage of your child's expected education costs you want to cover with savings.

- Start as soon as possible to save, and make the savings a regular habit (monthly is good).

- Use the tables above to calculate how much you need to set aside monthly to pay for your child's education.

Tim's Tip 27: Focus on equity investments and foreign content to improve returns over the long term.

If you're hoping to invest enough to cover all or a portion of your child's education costs, you'll want to maximize your investment returns within acceptable risk levels. This strategy will make the job of accumulating education funds that much easier. Let's look at the difference two percentage points can make. If you were to invest $2,000 annually for 18 years, generating a 6 percent annual return on your money, you'd have $65,520 at the end of that time. Increasing the rate of return from 6 to 8 percent over that time would result in an account worth $80,893 after 18 years. Increase the returns to 10 percent, and your assets would jump to $100,318 at the end of 18 years.

How do you maximize returns on investment? In two ways: by focusing on equity investments and by holding at least 40 percent of your investments in foreign content. You also need to consider which asset allocation is appropriate to get the job done.

Equities

Any investment adviser will tell you that, over the long term (typically five years), equity investments are likely to perform better than other investments—that is, interest-bearing investments. This is particularly true when you look at foreign stock markets (I'm going to talk about them in a minute). When I refer to equity investments, I'm talking primarily about stocks, or mutual funds that invest in stocks. Certainly some equities are higher risk than others. Resource and high–tech stocks, and mutual funds that invest in them, may be a higher risk than, say, a blue chip equity mutual fund that purchases shares in the largest corporations on the Toronto, New York, and other major stock exchanges.

Since you'll be investing for the long term in most cases when saving for education, equities are where you want to focus your investment dollars. The percentage of these equities that should be blue chip versus higher risk will depend on your tolerance for risk and the length of time before your child enrolls in postsecondary school. I'll talk more about this subject under the heading "Asset Allocation" below.

Action Step

If you've left the task of saving for your child's education to the last minute (within three years of your child attending college or university) and you're in a real bind, you may want to consider the option of investing some money in higher-risk equity investments that have the potential to increase significantly over the next couple of years. This option could provide your child with more than you might have expected in that first year of school. Of course, this option carries a greater downside potential too. Talk the issue over with a reputable financial adviser.

Foreign Content

It's a sad but true fact that foreign stock markets—notably U.S. markets—have outperformed Canada's equity markets over the long term. In addition, Canadian equity markets represent just under 3 percent of world markets, which tells me one thing— to neglect investing outside of Canada is to neglect some terrific investment opportunities. And when you're saving for your child's education, there is no restriction on foreign content as there is with your RRSP. That's right, RESPs and other, non-registered investment accounts are not subject to foreign content limits.

Your best bet, to maximize returns, is to hold at least 40 percent of the education savings of your child in foreign equity mutual funds. Many of Canada's mutual fund companies offer funds of foreign securities or funds tied to foreign stock markets.

Asset Allocation

So now you're focusing on equities and foreign markets. But any investment philosophy has to be adjusted from time to time. As your child gets older and approaches his first year of postsecondary education, you'll want to move to a slightly more conservative portfolio of investments, to reduce volatility at a time that is close to when your child will have to draw on those investments for school.

Here are three sample portfolios that make sense when saving for a child's education:

Newborn to Age 10: Aggressive

When your child is 10 or under, go for the gusto. Don't shy away from an aggressive portfolio. Focus on equity mutual funds as the core (at least 50 percent) of your portfolio, perhaps with individual stocks making up most of the balance. The assets in the portfolio could be allocated among the asset classes shown in the top pie chart.

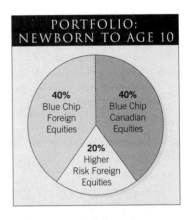

Age 11 to 14: Moderate

By the time your child is 11, it's time to shift investment gears slightly. Your objective at this stage is still growth, but at a more moderate risk level. Consider the asset allocation illustrated in the middle pie chart.

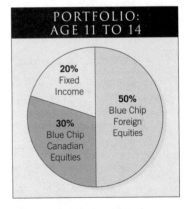

Age 15 to Graduation: Conservative

By this time, you've built up an education fund that you certainly don't want to subject to undue risk. You want the assets to be there when your child starts college or university! Keep in mind that you'll want to time the maturity of any fixed-income investments (bonds or mortgage-backed securities, for example) to coincide with the time your child will need cash to pay for education costs. Consider the asset allocation shown in the bottom pie chart.

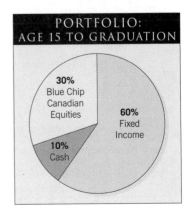

TO MAKE A LONG STORY SHORT:

- Maximizing investment returns can make a big difference in the amount of savings available to your child for education.

- To improve long-term investment returns, your asset allocation should focus mainly on equity investments, and at least 40 percent should be in foreign content.

- Consider choosing an asset allocation consistent with the three I've shown above, based on your child's age.

Tim's Tip 28: Stick to your investment strategy regardless of the "box" in which you hold your investments.

So far I haven't discussed RESPs, in-trust accounts, or other methods of saving for your child's education. All I've talked about here is *when* you should invest (as soon as possible and regularly), and *what types* of investments you should hold (equities and foreign content, with a shift in risk levels as your child gets older). Don't worry, I'll get to RESPs, in-trust accounts, and other such "boxes" for your investments in Chapters 5 and 6.

I look at RESPs and other investment accounts as boxes because they are vehicles in which to hold investments. Your first step is to decide *what types* of investments to hold (your asset allocation, discussed under the previous tip), and only then do you decide *where* to hold the investments (inside an RESP, in an in-trust account, or in a non-registered account for yourself).

For example, you might decide that your appropriate asset allocation is 40 percent foreign equities, 40 percent Canadian equities, 15 percent fixed income, and 5 percent cash. But do you hold these investments in an RESP, an in-trust account, an insurance policy, some other vehicle, or a combination of these boxes? That's a decision you'll be able to make once you've read Chapters 5 and 6.

Regardless of the box in which you choose to hold your investments, the investment strategy you have chosen should remain the same.

TO MAKE A LONG STORY SHORT:

- RESPs, in-trust accounts, insurance policies, and other vehicles to save for education are really just boxes in which to hold the investments you have chosen.

- The investment strategy you have chosen should remain the same, regardless of the box in which you choose to hold your investments.

WINNING THE EDUCATION SAVINGS GAME

Now you have a handle on the various ways to pay for an education: beg for free money, borrow, steal from your other resources, let your child sweat in the workforce to help cover the costs, and save for your child's education. The next step is to contemplate which of these is right for you and your child. In the next chapter, I'll help you pull these concepts together into a coherent education plan. Refer now to the Education Planning Tip Sheet at the front of the book to identify the tips you should make note of.

Did You Know?

A number of studies (most notably those by Brinson and Beebower) have shown that approximately 90 percent of all investment returns are determined by the asset allocation chosen for your money, not by the selection of specific securities. This is one more argument for sticking with your carefully considered asset allocation rather than moving your money from one investment to the next, hoping to find a "winner." This "stay-the-course" strategy works especially well over the long run, which is precisely the time frame you're likely dealing with when saving for a child's education.

WOODWORKING 101: BUILDING AN EDUCATION PLAN

Cauliflower is nothing but cabbage with a university education.

4

Judi and Ned decided to purchase a little cottage right on the ocean in Maine, close to where Ned grew up. Judi, Ned, Alexi, Zuri, and Samuel live in Boston, but they regularly make trips to Maine to visit Ned's parents, and they thought the cottage would be a quaint, quiet place to vacation.

The first weekend we spent at the cottage with Ned and Judi was anything but "quaint and quiet." "Quite the quagmire" would have been a better description. Only after buying the place did Ned and Judi discover that the septic system didn't work as advertised. We spent the better part of the weekend shoveling and mopping you-can-imagine-what from the floor of the cottage. Trust me, there wasn't an air freshener on the market that was up to the job that weekend.

This story had a happy ending, however. Two years and $20,000 later, Judi and Ned's place is as good as new. The smell is practically gone too.

Do you own a cottage? Have you dreamed of owning one? You know, I liken the purchase of a postsecondary education to the purchase of a cottage. First, an education costs a lot of money—about as much as most cottages you might hope to buy. Second, it makes a lot of sense to use the same buying tools and decision-making skills to purchase a college or university education that you would use to buy a cottage.

When you make a major purchase like a cottage, you have to identify the cash resources available to you. These resources might include savings, disposable income, investments, and perhaps a loan. You would no doubt take the time to determine how

Did You Know?

Obtaining information on the many schools your child is interested in can seem like a daunting task. Fortunately, the job is easier than ever today thanks to the Internet. Most colleges and universities have a presence on the Internet today, and finding a list of most of the schools is easy. Simply visit the Human Resources Development Canada Web site at www.youth.gc.ca/trainedu/univ_e.shtml for a thorough list of postsecondary institutions and links to their Web sites.

much the cottage is really going to cost, taking into consideration property taxes, utilities, insurance, and maintenance. Of course, before you actually buy the cottage of your dreams, you have to identify your dreams. That is, what are your goals? Why do you want to buy a cottage anyway? Do you want a place to get away from the city, to fix up for resale, or to develop into a retirement home?

Chances are pretty good that you would narrow your choice of a cottage to one or two properties. Then you'd assess which features are most important and try to determine which property would best meet your goals. Let's face it, it makes little sense to buy a cottage that needs no work at all when your objective is to buy a fixer-upper. Or, if your objective is to simply get away from the city on weekends, you probably wouldn't want to buy a place five hours away if you could find another one only two-and-a-half hours away that would meet your objective just as well.

The bottom line is, you want to buy a cottage that will meet your goals and fit your financial situation. If you have to take out a mortgage on the property, you recognize that you must have the ability to repay it. If you draw on your disposable income, you understand that you must still have enough income to meet your other living expenses.

The point here is that buying a postsecondary education involves more than just finding the funding for it. You want good value. Enter the education plan.

There are five steps to building a proper education plan. Determining how to pay for the education is the most critical, but not the only, step in the process. My intention is that by the time you finish reading this chapter, you will have developed an education plan to help your child find the right school and pay for it.

The five steps in the plan are as follows:
1. calculate the cost of your child's education
2. clarify your child's goals
3. compare and evaluate schools
4. choose your child's sources of funding
5. create your child's education plan

Documenting the Expected Costs

Tim's Tip 29: **Calculate the cost of your child's education as step 1 in building an education plan.**

We spent some time in Chapter 2 looking at the cost of education. You learned that it's on the rise. You'll recall that I introduced

Appendix A at that time. Appendix A contains tables that allow you to calculate what it's likely to cost to send your child to college or university in the future. You have to consider seven categories of expenses when determining the true cost of an education—the ones I introduced under Tip 6 in Chapter 2. I'll repeat them here:

- tuition and ancillary fees
- books and supplies
- accommodation
- food
- transportation
- personal care
- recreation and entertainment

The first step in creating an education plan is to get a handle on the education costs your child can expect. To help with this task, I've created an Education Cost Planner, shown on the following page. I recommend that you refer to Appendix A to help you complete this planner. Also, take a look at the sample planner that follows the Education Cost Planner. This sample has been completed for you.

TO MAKE A LONG STORY SHORT:

- The first step in building an education plan is to identify how much the education will cost.

- There are seven categories of expenses to consider. Completing the Education Cost Planner with the help of Appendix A at the back of this book should provide you with some guidance.

Clarifying Your Child's Goals

Tim's Tip 30: **Clarify your child's goals as step 2 in building an education plan.**

Now you've got a handle on the expected costs of your child's education. The next step is to talk with your child to determine her reasons

EDUCATION COST PLANNER						
Education Costs	Year 1	Year 2	Year 3	Year 4	Year 5	Total
Tuition and Ancillary Fees						
Tuition						
Student fees						
Special fees						
Subtotal						
Books and Supplies						
Books						
Supplies						
Computer/printer						
Subtotal						
Accommodation						
Residence on–campus						
Rent						
Utilities						
Subtotal						
Food						
Groceries						
Eating Out						
Subtotal						
Transportation						
Car expenses						
Insurance						
Airfare						
Bus fare						
Subtotal						
Personal Care						
Telephone						
Clothing/laundry						
Gifts						
Subscriptions/dues						
Other personal						
Child care						
Medical dental						
Subtotal						
Recreation and Entertainment						
Vacations						
Entertainment						
Extra–curricular						
Other						
Subtotal						
Total Education Costs						

EDUCATION COST PLANNER - SAMPLE						
Education Costs	**Year 1**	**Year 2**	**Year 3**	**Year 4**	**Year 5**	**Total**
Tuition and Ancillary Fees						
Tuition	$ 3,459	$ 3,771	$ 4,110	$ 4,480	$ –	$ 15,820
Student fees	250	272	297	324	–	1,143
Special fees	–	–	–	–	–	–
Subtotal	**3,709**	**4,043**	**4,407**	**4,804**	**–**	**16,963**
Books and Supplies						
Books	836	861	887	914	–	3,498
Supplies	400	412	424	437	–	1,673
Computer/printer	–	–	–	–	–	–
Subtotal	**1,236**	**1,273**	**1,311**	**1,351**	**–**	**5,171**
Accommodation						
Residence on–campus	–	–	–	–	–	–
Rent	3,296	3,395	3,497	3,602	–	13,790
Utilities	–	–	–	–	–	–
Subtotal	**3,296**	**3,395**	**3,497**	**3,602**	**–**	**13,790**
Food						
Groceries	1,142	1,176	1,212	1,248	–	4,778
Eating Out	300	309	318	328	–	1,255
Subtotal	**1,442**	**1,485**	**1,530**	**1,576**	**–**	**6,033**
Transportation						
Car expenses	–	–	–	–	–	–
Insurance	–	–	–	–	–	–
Airfare	–	–	–	–	–	–
Bus fare	1,030	1,061	1,093	1,126	–	4,310
Subtotal	**1,030**	**1,061**	**1,093**	**1,126**	**–**	**4,310**
Personal Care						
Telephone	400	412	424	437	–	1,673
Clothing/laundry	100	103	106	109	–	418
Gifts	200	206	212	219	–	837
Subscriptions/dues	25	26	27	27	–	105
Other personal	820	844	870	896	–	3,430
Child care	–	–	–	–	–	–
Medical dental	–	–	–	–	–	–
Subtotal	**1,545**	**1,591**	**1,639**	**1,688**	**–**	**6,463**
Recreation and Entertainment						
Vacations	–	–	–	–	–	–
Entertainment	675	695	716	738	–	2,824
Extra–curricular	200	206	212	219	–	837
Other	361	372	383	394	–	1,510
Subtotal	**1,236**	**1,273**	**1,311**	**1,351**	**–**	**5,171**
Total Education Costs	**13,494**	**14,121**	**14,788**	**15,498**	**–**	**57,901**

for pursuing a college or university education in the first place. What is it that you and she are trying to buy? What field of study does your child want to pursue? What does she hope to do after graduation?

It's important to understand what your child is looking to purchase when paying for this post-secondary education. Why? This information is critical to determining the schools to which your child should apply, and it will ultimately help guide her decision about which school to attend—assuming she has more than one choice in the matter, of course.

If your child is like many Canadian kids, she's not quite sure what she wants to do when she graduates. Setting goals can be difficult at this stage. If your child is in this boat, perhaps the best you can hope to accomplish is to help her narrow her focus. It's a good idea for your child to visit her high school guidance counsellor, who may have the right tools for this job.

It's not critical for a student to determine a final career path before college or university, but having some idea about interests, abilities, and values is important to allow the child to pursue an education program in which he is likely to enjoy himself—and excel. Human Resources Development Canada has all kinds of terrific tools available online to help you and your child find this direction. Check out the Web site www.youth.gc.ca/selfassess_e.shtml. Visiting this site and using these tools are highly recommended—even if your child has some comfort already about the area of study he'd like to pursue.

It's important that you let your child know that it's okay to be unsure about which field of study to pursue. In fact, college and university students change majors all the time. If your child really has trouble narrowing her focus to a particular area, her best bet is to enroll in general education courses that include one or two introductory courses to particular fields of study.

If your child really has difficulty narrowing her field of interest, it may make sense to delay enrollment at college or university for a while to allow her to explore the options available. Some experience in the working world might help her determine the potential career path that makes the most sense.

Here are some important questions that could trigger your child's thinking processes when she's attempting to clarify her goals:

Are You Pursuing an Education for Personal Fulfillment and Development?

- Is this the beginning of a new stage in life that will help to define who you really are?
- Is this your chance to pursue intellectual challenges?
- Do you want to gain independence by moving out of your home and establishing your own place?
- Is this simply a time for you to learn?

Are You Pursuing an Education to Improve Your Prospects for a Higher Income from Your Career?

- Have you decided on a career and need an education to achieve your dream?
- Do you know what kind of job you'd like after you graduate?
- Are the job prospects good for graduates in your chosen field of study?
- How much do you expect to earn after graduation?
- Is a university education the best route to your chosen field, or would a community college or vocational school better suit your needs?
- Do you work well with your hands? Have you considered an apprenticeship program, which is offered by many trades?

Are You Pursuing an Education to Acquire or Preserve Social Status?

• Do you want the best education available to improve your upward mobility?

• Are you intent on being associated with a particular college or university?

• Are you looking for particular initials or designations after your name for the prestige?

• Will college or university fulfill the expectations of your family or community?

TO MAKE A LONG STORY SHORT:

• The second step in building an education plan is to clarify your child's goals, which will help determine which school is best.

• This step requires you and your child to determine which field of study is most appropriate to help your child reach her goals.

Evaluating Different Schools

Tim's Tip 31: **Compare and evaluate schools to determine which one is best, as step 3 in building an education plan.**

It's time to shop around for the right school. I've provided a School Evaluation Summary on page 90 to be completed by your child. You can help by lending your child a hand when he needs to call a particular school for information, or by checking written materials or the school's Web site for answers to specific questions.

When the summary is complete, it can provide a good basis for evaluating and ranking schools. There's a place on the summary for your child to add specific questions that are not already listed. Make maximum use of this space! Your child might have questions about the sports offered at the school, the proximity of the school to shopping or movies, and so on.

Here's a list of the criteria that your child should use to evaluate his top choices for an educational institution:

1. *Field of study.* Does this college or university have a program ideally suited to helping you achieve your academic goals?
2. *Education costs.* When you factor in all categories of costs, is this school affordable?
3. *Financial assistance.* Does the school offer free money in the form of scholarships, awards, bursaries, or the like that you are eligible to receive?
4. *Job opportunities.* Does the school provide opportunities to find a job on campus? Are there plenty of jobs available in the community around the school? How much can a student earn at these jobs?
5. *Cooperative education program.* Does the school offer a co-op program to allow you to work in your field of study to gain experience and earn income?
6. *Jobs after graduation.* How successful are graduates of the school in finding high-paying work related to their field of study? Are any statistics available about graduates, such as median incomes or placement rates?
7. *Extracurricular activities.* Are there opportunities for involvement at the school in clubs, groups, and the like, to enhance the experience of attending the school?

SCHOOL EVALUATION SUMMARY					
Criteria	**School 1**	**School 2**	**School 3**	**School 4**	**School 5**
1. Field of study					
2. Education costs					
3. Financial assistance					
4. Job opportunity					
5. Co-op program					
6. Job after graduation					
7. Extra-curricular activities					
8. Cost cutters					
9. Other					
10. Other					
Total score					

Instruction: For each school on your list, provide a score for the school between 1 and 5 on each of the criteria listed, where 1= downright bad, 2= needs improvement, 3= good, 4= very good, and 5= outstanding. Then add up all the numbers for each school to provide an overall score for the school.

8. *Cost cutters.* Can you live at home and commute to the school? Will the school grant credits for prior life experience, independent study, or correspondence courses? Does the school offer free parking? Does the school provide free access to the Internet or any other important services?

TO MAKE A LONG STORY SHORT:

- Evaluating and ranking the schools of choice should be done by your child. This work can be done by examining the criteria in the School Evaluation Summary worksheet.

- Have your child take a look at *Maclean's* latest university rankings—the magazine's Web site address is www.macleans.ca—to help him complete the School Evaluation Summary.

Designing a Funding Plan

Tim's Tip 32: **Choose your child's sources of funding as step 4 in building an education plan.**

Chapter 3 was devoted to explaining the five methods of paying for a postsecondary education—begging, borrowing, stealing, sweating, and saving. Now it's time to decide which of these sources your child will use to pay for that education. To evaluate these options properly, you need to understand that each of these alternatives has an underlying assumption. Once you understand the assumptions, you will find it easier to decide which sources of funding are right for your child. The assumptions are as follows:

Source of Funding	Assumption
Begging	Assumes qualifications and persistence
Borrowing	Assumes ability to repay
Stealing	Assumes available resources
Sweating	Assumes time and skill
Saving	Assumes time and income

Begging

Your child is not likely to raise enough money to attend three or four years of postsecondary school by begging, unless she excels in an area that qualifies her for scholarships, has a financial need that could lead to grants, or qualifies because of her field of study or research. And it takes more than qualifications. It takes persistence. There are plenty of qualified candidates out there. Who's going to get the free money? If qualifications are in the bag, then persistence should pay off.

Borrowing

If your child borrows money, you have to assume that she will have the ability to pay it back. Borrowing for an education should be based on future earnings expectations. If you have little or no confidence that your child will have the income to repay a loan, then discourage her from borrowing in the first place. To make an educated guess as to the likelihood that your child will be able to handle the loan payments, you're going to need some idea of the employment prospects for those graduating in her field.

How much should your child borrow? Good question. The answer is not necessarily "as much as she can get her hands on." I suggest that you follow the Rule of Tens—for every $10,000 in student loans, your child should earn about $10,000 annually over a base income of $10,000 in order to repay the loans in 10 years.

Here's what I mean. If your child graduates with student loans of $30,000, then she ought to earn $30,000 a year plus a base of $10,000, for a total of $40,000 annually, to be able to pay off that loan in 10 years. And this level of income should be the minimum.

Once your child is out of school and working full-time, she'll have to maintain a tight lid on the amount of money she borrows over and above her student loans, especially if her student loan payments amount to more than 25 percent of her gross salary. If your child lets her debt get out of control, it may make sense to consolidate the debt into one loan if the interest rate on the loan is reasonable. If credit cards are the culprit, tell your child to cut them up. If it's necessary for her to have credit, she should have one card only, and she should put it in a glass of water in the freezer. That way, she'll have to think twice before using it!

Caution!

REQUIRED SALARY BASED ON STUDENT DEBT		
Student Debt	**Annual Salary**	**Monthly Payment**
$ 10,000	$ 20,000	$ 127
15,000	25,000	190
20,000	30,000	253
25,000	35,000	317
30,000	40,000	380
40,000	50,000	507
50,000	60,000	633

Assumptions:
– interest rate of 9% per annum
– term of loan is 10 years

Even at this level, 11.4 percent of your child's gross income will be devoted to paying off student debt over 10 years. While that may not sound like a high percentage, it is.

Check out the following table for an idea of how much income your child should earn, as a minimum, for different levels of student debt. I've included the monthly payments required to clear the debt in 10 years.

When formulating your child's education funding plan, it's important to consider how much debt is too much.

Stealing

If you plan to steal from your other resources, you're making the assumption that you will have resources from which to steal. You'll recall from Tips 20 and 21 that I discourage folks from stealing and liquidating their lifestyle assets (cars, boats, cottages, collections) to pay for a child's education. I'm even more adamant that you leave your retirement assets (RRSPs and other retirement savings) untouched.

If you're going to steal from your other resources, make sure these resources consist primarily of disposable income, a line of credit, and non-retirement investments. Do you have these resources available to you today? How available are they likely to be when your child enters college or university? You'll need to make an educated guess as to whether you'll have resources from which to steal.

Sweating

Encouraging your child to sweat to pay for education assumes that she has the time and skill to work in a job that will contribute money to this purpose. How many hours a week can she work while still maintaining that 3.0 grade point average? Don't forget, your child's first priority, if she is enrolling full-time, is to hit the books. If work interferes with studying and learning, then work defeats the purpose of attending school.

As I said under Tip 25 in the last chapter, 15 hours of work each week should be the maximum for a full-time student. Beyond that level, your child's ability to score good grades is likely to be affected.

Some students (or their parents!) might decide that working more and taking fewer courses is best. This is an option, but remember, the longer it takes to graduate, the more future income is forgone, since it will take your child longer to reach her maximum earning potential. A cooperative study program, however, could make sense for those students who really want to combine work and study (see Tip 23).

Saving

Setting aside money today for the future when your child attends college or university assumes that you have time enough for that money to grow and that you have the disposable income today to set up a savings program.

Don't misunderstand. I'm not suggesting that if your child is already 16 years of age and will be attending university in two years that you should dismiss any plan to save, simply because two years isn't a lot of time for the money to grow. What I am suggesting is that to make this strategy as effective as possible, you should start as early as possible, since time is critical to growing assets.

Disposable income is another issue. Maybe you're starting to save for your first home, for a business you hope to start, or for some other reason. If this is the case, you'll need to assess your priorities. Where in your scale of priorities is setting aside money today for your child's education? Hey, if you plan for your child's education to be paid for through begging, borrowing, stealing, and sweating, then it may not be so important to save.

But remember, saving for your child's education has one key advantage over the other methods of financing your child's education—saving is a sure thing. No matter what, if you set up a proper savings program, you will have a pot of money for your child's education at the end of the rainbow. None of the other sources are as reliable. For this reason alone, it's important, if possible, to set aside money for your child's education.

TO MAKE A LONG STORY SHORT:

- You have to decide which combination of the five funding strategies—begging, borrowing, stealing, sweating, and saving—will finance your child's education.

- Each of these sources of funding assumes certain things about you and your child. Understand these assumptions before deciding which source you'll use.

- Saving is the only sure thing. The other sources of funding involve an element of uncertainty.

Visualizing the Education Plan

Tim's Tip 33: **Create a visual format of your child's plan as step 5 in building an education plan.**

I like this step of building an education plan the best. My wife says it's because my favourite part of kindergarten was drawing. Maybe there's a kernel of truth buried there, but I think I really enjoy this last step of the process because it's the end of the line. That is, when you get here you will have arrived at a tentative game plan for paying for your child's education. Things could change between now and the time your child darkens the doors of Sociology 101, but the plan can easily be modified.

I also firmly believe that *seeing* a visual image of how the cost of education will be met represents a giant leap towards actually making it happen. In fact, I'm going to suggest *two* visual aids. Both will provide you with a glimpse of the future. The first tool is the Education Planning Chart, the second is the Education Planning Pyramid. Take a look at them on the following page.

Filling in the chart and pyramid is easy. Follow these instructions:

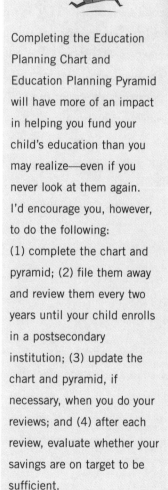

Action Step

Completing the Education Planning Chart and Education Planning Pyramid will have more of an impact in helping you fund your child's education than you may realize—even if you never look at them again. I'd encourage you, however, to do the following: (1) complete the chart and pyramid; (2) file them away and review them every two years until your child enrolls in a postsecondary institution; (3) update the chart and pyramid, if necessary, when you do your reviews; and (4) after each review, evaluate whether your savings are on target to be sufficient.

- Complete the Education Planning Chart first. Enter the expected costs of your child's education for each year (refer back to Tip 29 for the expected costs). Next, enter the dollar amount to be raised through each of the sources—begging, borrowing, stealing, sweating, and saving. I've provided a sample of a completed Education Planning Chart, following the case study (example).

- The Education Planning Pyramid is next. Draw horizontal lines across the pyramid to represent each of the sources of funding that you have chosen and documented in the Education Planning Chart. The Education Planning Pyramid has marks indicating area percentages. Use these marks as a guide in estimating the portions to be filled by begging, borrowing, stealing, sweating, and saving. Again, check out the sample Education Planning Pyramid following the case study.

EDUCATION PLANNING CHART – SAMPLE							
	Year 1	Year 2	Year 3	Year 4	Year 5	Total	Percentage of Total
Expected Education Costs	$ 23,116	$ 24,384	$ 25,741	$ 27,196	$ –	$ 100,437	100.0%
Beg	500	500	500	500	–	2,000	2.0%
Borrow	5,000	5,000	5,000	5,000	–	20,000	19.9%
Steal	3,000	4,000	5,000	5,000	–	17,000	16.9%
Sweat	5,000	5,200	5,500	6,000	–	21,700	21.6%
Save	9,616	9,684	9,741	10,696	–	39,737	39.6%
Total	$ 23,116	$ 24,384	$ 25,741	$ 27,196	$ –	$ 100,437	100.0%

*J*anice and Peter have been contemplating how they're going to help their daughter Tori, now age 7, pay for an education. The couple completed the Education Planning Chart under the assumption that Tori will attend her first year of postsecondary school in 2011. (They estimated the cost of each year of her education by completing the Education Cost Planner, way back under Tip 29, step 1.)

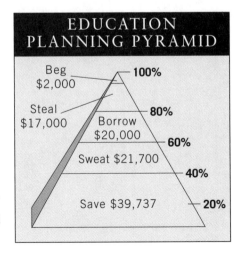

EDUCATION PLANNING CHART							
	Year 1	Year 2	Year 3	Year 4	Year 5	Total	Percentage of Total
Expected Education Costs							
Beg							
Borrow							
Steal							
Sweat							
Save							
Total							

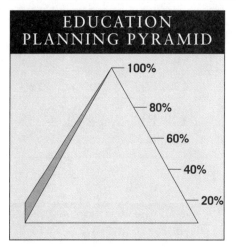

EDUCATION PLANNING PYRAMID

Janice and Peter evaluated the sources of money available to them and the assumptions underlying each source. After carefully considering their options, they decided that their education plan for Tori will include begging, borrowing, stealing, sweating, and saving. That is, they plan to make use of all the sources of funding. Working with the visual aids, they developed the following plan.

The base of Tori's Education Planning Pyramid will be saving. Janice and Peter figure they have time to save for Tori's education, since she's just 7 years old. In fact, they have already set aside some money. They also feel they can manage to find enough disposable income on a monthly basis to save to cover $39,737, or 39.5 percent, of Tori's education costs. The couple expects Tori to sweat for $21,700—21.6 percent—of her education costs, and to borrow $20,000—20 percent. They plan to kick in an *extra $17,000, or 16.9 percent, through stealing from non-retire-ment investments they already have. Finally, they expect that Tori will be eligible for some free money, to the tune of $2,000, or 2 percent, of her total education costs.*

TO MAKE A LONG STORY SHORT:

• The fifth and final step in building an education plan is creating the plan in a visual format.

• Seeing the plan in the form of the Education Planning Chart and the Education Planning Pyramid will make it much easier to attain the goal of ensuring that the cost of your child's education will be met.

WINNING THE EDUCATION SAVINGS GAME

My father-in-law, Burt, says that if you want to make sure your spouse listens intently to everything you say and never interrupts you when you speak, just talk in your sleep. By now you've heard about the sources of education funding so many times you're probably talking about them in your sleep. I hope so. It means that you understand the concept of begging, borrowing, stealing, sweating, and saving for your child's education. I also hope that by now you've completed the Education Planning Chart and Education Planning Pyramid. If so, congratulate yourself, you're well on your way to funding your child's education. Now, turn to the Education Planning Tip Sheet at the front and check off those tips that you'd like to make a note of.

TOP OF THE CLASS: THE NEW RESP AND CESG

Why plough a field with a rake when you've got the right tools?

5

What a beautiful day it was, July 17 last summer. Twenty-six degrees, sunny, and best of all, I was up by two strokes on my brother-in-law Peter, which is a rare thing. He usually beats me at golf. We were on the 12th hole—at Glen Abbey in Oakville, no less. On his last tee shot, Peter created a divot big enough to require the laying of a new roll of sod. The divot reminded me a little of Mr. Crabchuk's hair. Mr. Crabchuk was a teacher in my high school who had a ton of hair. I bet he kept it in his drawer at night. His toupee was not unlike Peter's divot.

Peter is a high school teacher himself. In addition to discussing Mr. Crabchuk's toupee, we talked about the large number of times education-related news has hit the headlines in the last year or two. Here are some headlines that caught my eye:

- "Local High School Dropouts Cut in Half"
- "Safety Experts Say School Bus Passengers Should Be Belted"
- "Old School Pillars Are Replaced by Alumni"
- "Sex Education Delayed, Teachers Request Training."
  But Not All the Headlines Were Bloopers. Check These Out:
- "Federal Budget Broadens RESPs,"
  Globe and Mail, February 28, 1998
- "Tax-Deductible or Not, RESPs Are Hot,"
  Winnipeg Free Press, August 8, 1998
- "Flexibility, Grants Raise RESP Appeal,"
  National Post, November 20, 1998
- "Rule Changes Add to RESP Allure,"
  Globe and Mail, December 2, 1998
- "The Many Virtues of the Remodelled RESP,"
  Toronto Star, December 10, 1998
- "RESPs Winning Favour Among Canadians,"
  Lethbridge Herald, December 19, 1998
- "Grant Gives RESPs New Personality,"
  London Free Press, January 30, 1999
- "RESPs a Good Recipe for Continued Education,"
  Calgary Sun, March 7, 1999
- "Students Win Tax Breaks from Ottawa,"
  Toronto Sun, April 19, 1999.

Get the drift? Registered education savings plans (RESPs) have changed recently, particularly as a result of the 1997 and 1998 federal budgets. There are new rules and the new RESP looks better than ever.

In Chapter 4 we spent some time putting together a plan to pay for your child's education. I made the point that saving for a child's education (as opposed to begging, borrowing, stealing, or sweating) is the surest way of paying for school.

Now, there are a number of ways to save for a child's education. You could simply stuff some money under your mattress. Or you could deposit it in a bank account, open an in-trust account, use a life insurance policy, or use an RESP, among other options. In this chapter, I want to focus on RESPs and the related Canada Education Savings Grants (CESGs).

We will spend some time in Chapters 6 and 7 talking about the other ways of saving for education (except stuffing money under your mattress, which you can probably figure out on your own). But I've dedicated this chapter exclusively to RESPs and CESGs because there's a lot to say and because I'm a firm believer that any savings or investing component of your education savings plan should include an RESP. I'll explain why in just a minute, in Tip 34.

Before we jump into it, let me warn you that I may not answer every question you might have about RESPs and CESGs in this chapter. I've devoted Chapter 8 to that task. In Chapter 8, I pose and answer 99 questions on RESPs, CESGs, and related stuff. My objective in this chapter is simply to introduce RESPs and CESGs, and share with you some tips on how to make the most of them. Now, let's hop to it.

Understanding the New RESP

If you're going to make the best use of RESPs, you first need to understand a bit about them, and then heed the advice I provide below. You'll find that your RESP dollar will go farther this way.

Tim's Tip 34: **Make an RESP a part of any education savings program.**

We could debate until the cows come home—or until your child leaves home, whichever comes first—about whether you should use an RESP to save for your child's education, but let's not. Let me ward off that debate by saying that an RESP doesn't need to be your *only* means of saving, but it should form the cornerstone of any carefully planned education strategy. Here are several reasons why:

- An RESP can provide a boost to your education savings plan by making use of the Canada Education Savings Grants (CESGs) available from Ottawa. (I'll talk more about the CESG soon).
- An RESP offers 100 percent guaranteed tax-free compounding inside the plan.
- No annual tax filings are required with an RESP, which makes these plans simple to administer once set up.
- RESPs can provide all the investment choices you'll ever really need to effectively save for an education.
- It's possible to claim a refund of your contributions to the plan, if you want to.
- RESPs are more flexible now, allowing you some practical alternatives if your child doesn't enroll in a qualifying educational program.
- RESPs allow for income-splitting, since the accumulated income in the plan will

While I'm a firm believer that an RESP should be part of every education savings program, don't make the mistake of assuming that this rules out other alternatives, like an in-trust account. RESPs and in-trust accounts are not mutually exclusive ways to save for a child's education. There's absolutely nothing wrong with having both of these tools working for you. Choosing one to the exclusion of the other could mean you're not making the most of your savings opportunities. Stay tuned, as I'll talk more about in-trust accounts in Tip 52 and in Chapter 8.

Caution!

be taxed in the beneficiary's hands when paid out as educational assistance payments.

• RESPs offer a couple of psychological advantages: They have a contribution deadline each December 31, which adds a sense of urgency about contributing, and the plans must have a specific purpose, which discourages you or your child from using the funds for other things.

TO MAKE A LONG STORY SHORT:

• An RESP doesn't need to be your only means of saving for a child's education, but it should be the cornerstone of an effective education savings strategy.

• RESPs are attractive for many reasons, the most significant of which is the opportunity to receive grants—CESGs—from the government.

Tim's Tip 35: Understand the basics about RESPs before subscribing to a plan.

I'm a firm believer that you shouldn't make use of any investment vehicle unless you understand it pretty thoroughly. You avoid unpleasant surprises this way. If I could pinpoint the 10 critical things you need to know about RESPs, they would be as follows:

1. *Parties to the RESP.* As a contributor to an RESP you're known as the "subscriber." The person for whom you've set up the plan (the future student) is the "beneficiary." The financial institution or firm through which you set up the RESP is known as the "promoter."

2. *Contribution limits.* The subscriber can contribute up to $4,000 each year to an RESP for each beneficiary, with a lifetime maximum of $42,000 per beneficiary.

3. *Tax benefits.* You don't receive a tax deduction for contributions to an RESP, but the assets in the plan can compound tax-free over the years.

4. *Beneficiaries' tax situation.* The student beneficiary will be taxed on the accumulated income in the plan when it is withdrawn for educational purposes as "educational assistance payments."

5. *Duration of an RESP.* An RESP can exist for 25 years, after which time it must be terminated. While the plan can exist for 25 years, contributions can only be made for the first 21 years of the plan. (See question 3 in Chapter 8 for more information.)

6. *Refund of contributions.* The subscriber is permitted to withdraw tax free at any time any contributions made to the plan. (An RESP promoter may place restrictions on withdrawals, however, even though our tax law allows them).

7. *Types of RESPs.* There are two types of RESPs—self-directed plans and group plans. Self-directed plans are generally more flexible, since they allow the subscriber to control investment decisions and the timing of payments out of the plan, whereas group plans (sometimes referred to as pooled plans) offered by scholarship trust organizations generally provide little or no discretion in these matters. I'll talk more about both types of plans in Tip 36.

8. *Individual and family plans.* Self-directed and group plans can be divided into two subtypes of plans—individual plans and multi-beneficiary plans, which are commonly known as family plans. An individual plan is permitted just one beneficiary. A multi-beneficiary plan can have more than one beneficiary, but each beneficiary must be connected to the subscriber by blood or adoption. I'll discuss these plans in more detail in Tip 37.

9. *Transfers between plans.* Transfers can generally be made from one RESP to another on a tax-free basis. Complications can arise in certain situations (see question 4 in Chapter 8).

10. *Options if beneficiary rejects school.* If a plan beneficiary does not enroll in a qualifying educational program, the subscriber can

do one of six things: (1) name a new beneficiary under the plan; (2) allocate the accumulated income to other beneficiaries already in the plan; (3) transfer the plan assets to another RESP with different beneficiaries (with some restrictions); (4) roll up to $50,000 of RESP assets into his (the subscriber's) RRSP, provided he has sufficient RRSP contribution room; (5) donate the accumulated income in the plan to a college or university; or (6) withdraw the contributions (called a "refund of payments") and accumulated income (called "accumulated income payments") from the plan for himself.

The accumulated income payments in the last option are fully taxable for the subscriber, and a 20 percent penalty tax will apply to those payments as well. Before you can receive an accumulated income payment or roll the RESP accumulated income to an RRSP, the plan has to have been in existence for at least 10 years and all beneficiaries must be age 21 and ineligible to receive educational assistance payments from the plan.

TO MAKE A LONG STORY SHORT:

- Make sure you understand the basics about RESPs before opening a plan.

Did You Know?

The Cathedral of Learning at the University of Pittsburgh is the tallest school building in the Western world, standing at 535 feet (42 storeys). Built in Gothic style between 1926 and 1937, it houses unique Nationality Classrooms, and 23 authentically designed and decorated classrooms developed and funded by the ethnic communities of the Pittsburgh area. Some classrooms were made completely in their home countries, disassembled and shipped to the University to be put back together again.

- Ten key points are involved. I will discuss these points in more depth in the question-and-answer session in Chapter 8.

Tim's Tip 36: **Learn to recognize the two types of RESPs.**

It can be tough, when you're reading all the literature and hearing all the marketing pitches about RESPs, to understand the different types of plans. But, as I pointed out above, RESPs can be broken down into two general types—self-directed plans and group plans. There are four fundamental differences between self-directed and group plans:

- investment alternatives
- timing and amount of payouts permitted
- ability to change beneficiaries
- education program requirements.

Let's take a closer look at the two types of RESPs.

Self-Directed Plans

A self-directed RESP may sound a little intimidating—as though you've got to do a lot of work yourself. In fact, these plans are called self-directed because you are able to control (or "direct") the types of investments you hold in them. And the investment options can be as varied as the options for RRSPs, including mutual funds, stocks, bonds, guaranteed investment certificates (GICs), and much more. (See a more complete list in Tip 44.)

In addition to investment flexibility, self-directed plans also come with flexibility in other areas. The most important area may be the timing of payouts to the RESP's beneficiaries. For the most part, you can choose how much the beneficiaries should receive from the plan, and when. The only restriction the government imposes is a limit of $5,000 on withdrawals made in the first 13 weeks of a qualifying program. After that 13-week period, your payout options are usually wide open. You could even pay out every cent of the plan all at once, if you wanted to.

A self-directed plan also provides the most flexibility when it comes to a change in the beneficiaries of the plan (see question 37 in Chapter 8), a transfer of the plan's assets to another RESP (question 4 in Chapter 8), or the duration of qualifying educational programs (question 46 in Chapter 8).

Group Plans

Group plans are not nearly as flexible as self-directed plans. Group plans are sometimes referred to as "pooled trust plans," and they are offered by a few scholarship trust organizations in Canada. (You'll find a list of the most prominent scholarship trust organizations in Appendix B.)

When you open a group RESP, you're really entering into a contract in which you agree to buy a certain number of shares, or "units," and to pay for those units over a period of time. The scholarship trust organization will pool your money with that of the other subscribers and invest it in very secure investments. You have no say in how the money is invested. These group plans are restricted to investing in government-guaranteed or -insured investments like government bonds, Treasury bills, mortgage-backed securities, and GICs—as you can see, the investment options are pretty limited. And as I pointed out earlier (see Tip 27 in Chapter 3), rates of return on these types of interest-bearing investments have been lower over the long term than they have been on equity investments.

Let's consider payouts from a group plan. You'll commonly find that any contributions you make to the RESP are returned to you (minus fees and administrative charges) once your child starts her postsecondary education. The idea is that you will use this capital to contribute to your child's first year of school. The accumulated income in the plan will then be paid out as "scholarships" over the remaining years of your child's schooling. If you were hoping that your child could withdraw all the RESP assets in the first year of postsecondary school, think again. Group plans don't offer this kind of flexibility.

The amount of the total payments to your child over the course of her education is determined by three things: (1) interest rates (the higher the rates, the more money earned in the plan, and the more available to be paid out); (2) subscribers who stop contributing (if a subscriber stops contributing to the plan before it matures, any contributions he has made are likely to be returned to him, and the accumulated income on those contributions will be split among the remaining beneficiaries in the plan); and (3) the number of beneficiaries who choose not to attend postsecondary school (kids who go this route will usually forfeit the accumulated income in the plan, which will be split among the beneficiaries still in the plan).

Unlike under a self-directed plan, your ability to name a new beneficiary under a group RESP usually exists for a short time only, often only until the child is age 12 (although some plans may now extend this age limit).

Finally, it's critical under most group plans that the child enroll in a qualifying educational program for at least two years. A one-year program won't cut it. Your child is likely to forfeit any accumulated income in the plan if she doesn't enroll in a program of two years or more.

Let me make one more comment here about scholarship trust organizations. Some of these companies now offer self-directed plans that are more flexible than their traditional group plans. In some cases, however, what they call a self-directed plan (or a "self-determined" or "self-initiated" plan) is really nothing more than a group plan with some added flexibility.

In the end, it's doubtful that these plans are as flexible as a true self-directed plan.

For example, I'm not aware of any scholarship trust that will allow the subscriber to take the accumulated income out of the plan as an accumulated income payment (see Tip 38, point 3) if the beneficiary chooses not to attend school. The reason, I suspect, is that a group plan is a trust arrangement where the subscriber transfers title over the accumulated interest to the trustee. The subscriber in this case doesn't have the option of taking possession of the accumulated income in the plan, as he would under a true self-directed plan.

TO MAKE A LONG STORY SHORT:

- There are two basic types of RESPs—self-directed plans and group plans. Self-directed plans generally offer much more flexibility than group plans.

- Scholarship trust organizations offer group plans, and they may also promote self-directed plans. But beware! It's doubtful that these "self-directed" plans are as flexible as those available elsewhere.

Tim's Tip 37: **Consider opting for an individual plan over a family plan.**

As you already know, from the list of 10 critical points about RESPs that I provided in Tip 35, both self-directed and group plans can be broken down further into two sub-types of plans—individual plans

Some scholarship trust organizations now offer self-directed plans that are more flexible than their traditional group plans. In some cases, however, what they call a self-directed (or a "self-determined" or "self-initiated" plan) is really nothing more than a group plan with some added flexibility. In the end, it's doubtful that these plans are as flexible as a true self-directed plan. For example, I'm not aware of any scholarship trust that will allow the subscriber to take the accumulated income as an accumulated income payment (see Tip 38, point 3) if the beneficiary chooses not to attend school.

Caution!

and family plans. Once you've decided on a self-directed or group plan, you then have to decide whether that plan will be an individual plan or a family plan.

Both individual plans and family plans work very much the same way, and they have all the characteristics of RESPs that I spoke about in Tip 34. There are, however, four key differences between individual and family plans:

- An individual plan cannot have more than one beneficiary, while a family plan can. (Family plans are also called "multi-beneficiary" plans.)
- A family plan will allow you to allocate the accumulated income in the RESP to any of the beneficiaries in any proportion. So if one beneficiary does not opt for a postsecondary education, the accumulated income can be used by the others.
- An individual plan will allow you to name a beneficiary of any age, while a family plan requires that all beneficiaries be under age 21 at the time they become beneficiaries.
- You can name absolutely anyone (including yourself or your spouse) as a beneficiary under an individual plan, while a family plan requires that all the beneficiaries be connected to the subscriber by blood or adoption (see question 5 in Chapter 8 for more details).

Which plan is better for you and your family—an individual plan or a family plan? It's commonly felt that a family plan makes lots of sense, since you can name all your children as beneficiaries, and if one of them doesn't go to school, you can allow the others to utilize the accumulated income in the plan for their schooling. Under a family plan, you don't really lose anything if at least one child pursues a postsecondary education.

But I'm going to buck the trend here and put in a vote for individual plans. I like individual plans for the following reasons:

- It's possible with an individual plan to name a beneficiary who is over age 21. This is not possible under a family plan. This feature can provide more flexibility down the road if you want to name a new beneficiary.

- It's also possible with an individual plan to name a beneficiary who is not related by blood or adoption. For example, you, your spouse, a niece or nephew, or a family friend could be named as beneficiary if your child decides not to attend school. (I discuss the "blood or adoption" relationship in question 5 in Chapter 8.) Again, this feature simply provides added flexibility later if you want to change beneficiaries.

- You can name your own child as beneficiary of the individual plan (one plan for each child), and if it appears that one of your children will not be pursuing an education, it's easy to transfer the assets from that RESP to the others on a tax-free basis (see question 4 in Chapter 8 for more on transfers).

- Alternatively, with an individual plan you could simply remove your "truant" child (the one who's passing up an education) as beneficiary and add your other children as beneficiaries (see question 37 in Chapter 8 for more information on changing beneficiaries).

- If you have separate individual plans for each of your kids, you can even transfer all the assets from each of the individual plans into a family plan at a later date, provided all beneficiaries are still under age 21.

With a family plan, you'll only pay one administration fee each year, since you're only dealing with one plan. This is not the case if you open

Did You Know?

The University of Calgary offers a two-day course in igloo building. There's a course taught at the University at Buffalo on the life and works of Frank Zappa. Ballroom dancing is a major at Brigham Young University. The world's first college course about radio personality Rush Limbaugh is taught at Bellevue University in Nebraska. And, North America's only bachelor's degree in bagpiping is taught at Carnegie Mellon University in Pittsburgh.

a separate individual plan for each child. But provided you're willing to pay the additional administration fees associated with a second and third RESP, and provided you're willing to take the time to change beneficiaries or transfer plan assets if one child chooses not to attend school, then I like the individual plans better.

Here's a final point: There's an important difference between setting up an individual plan and setting up a family plan with just one beneficiary. The family plan, even if it has just one beneficiary, will contain age (under age 21) and relationship (connected by blood or adoption) restrictions on who can become a beneficiary in the future. Don't let your financial institution or adviser sell you a family plan if you really want an individual plan!

TO MAKE A LONG STORY SHORT:

- Self-directed and group RESPs can be broken down into two types of plans: individual and family plans.

- I like individual plans better because they offer more flexibility if you want to change beneficiaries later. But make sure you understand the rules about making transfers between plans and changing beneficiaries (see questions 4 and 37 in Chapter 8).

- You can always combine individual plans later into a family plan, provided the age (under age 21) and relationship (connected by blood or adoption) conditions for family plans are met.

Tim's Tip 38: **Understand the four types of withdrawals from an RESP.**

RESP withdrawals can be split into four basic types, and each has its own tax implications:

1. *Refund of payments.* You may remember from Tip 35 that a

subscriber to an RESP is entitled to withdraw her original contributions, free of tax. These withdrawals are called a "refund of payments." Most plans will allow a refund of payments at any time, but some group plans may place restrictions on them. Check with your RESP promoter.

2. *Educational assistance payments (EAPs).* EAPs are the payments made from the RESP to your child to assist with his education costs. These are not the same thing as the tax-free refund of payments referred to in point 1 above. Rather, EAPs represent the income that has accumulated inside the RESP and that is therefore taxable in the hands of the child.

3. *Accumulated income payments (AIPs).* An AIP is the payment of the accumulated income in the RESP to the *subscriber* when the beneficiary of the RESP does not pursue a qualifying educational program. The accumulated income can be paid out as an EAP to the beneficiary if the beneficiary goes to school, or as an AIP (to the subscriber) if the beneficiary has reached age 21, is not pursuing an education, and the

Action Step

The withdrawal of accumulated income in the RESP by the subscriber should be done only as a last resort—a desperation move, you might say. Since the subscriber will pay tax on the accumulated income payment, plus a 20 percent penalty, it's an ugly option. If it's obvious your child won't be enrolling in postsecondary education, consider one of the other options I talked about in Tip 35, point 10, before deciding to take accumulated income payments. Specifically, try to name a new beneficiary on the plan, allocate the assets to other beneficiaries in the plan, transfer the assets to another plan or roll the assets to an RRSP if possible.

plan has existed for 10 years. An AIP is taxed in the hands of the subscriber, and is subject to an additional 20 percent penalty unless the assets are rolled into the subscriber's RRSP (see Tip 41 on transfers to an RRSP). Here's an important point: Once an AIP has been paid out of an RESP, the plan must be terminated before March of the following year.

4. *Transfers to another RESP.* This is the fourth type of withdrawal. Generally, there are no tax consequences to a transfer from one RESP to another (see question 4 in Chapter 8 for more information on transfers).

Considering Specific RESP Strategies

Tim's Tip 39: Be sure to ask the critical questions before choosing a particular plan.

Not all RESPs are created equal. In fact, RESP promoters may offer you all kinds of features under our tax law, but they may choose not to offer them. To help you evaluate plans against one another, I've come up with seven questions that you should ask an RESP promoter before buying into a particular RESP. You may find big differences between plans.

1. *Can I control the timing of payments out of the plan when my child begins postsecondary school?* In an ideal world, you would have complete control over the timing of these payments to the beneficiaries. Some plans, particularly group plans, may place some restrictions on the timing of payments. The government places only one restriction on the timing of withdrawals: During the first 13 weeks of an educational program, the total payments from an RESP cannot exceed $5,000. After 13 weeks, this restriction is gone.

2. *Can the full value of the plan be withdrawn in the first year of school?* Some plans may provide you with some, but not complete, flexibility to choose the timing of withdrawals. (Many group plans work this way.) Most notably, some plans may require that funds be left in the RESP for withdrawal each year that the child is enrolled in a qualifying educational program. The most flexible plans will allow your child to make withdrawals at any time, and even to withdraw all the funds in the first year. Be sure to ask the question.

3. *Can I claim a refund of my contributions to the RESP any time I want to?* Some promoters may restrict the timing of your ability as the subscriber to take back a refund of the contributions you made to the plan. The most flexible plans won't restrict the timing of these withdrawals.

4. *Can I control the investment decisions for assets inside the plan?* Ask the promoter what

Action Step

Most group RESPs are sold through sales people or agents who typically make hundreds of cold calls and solicit the business of friends and family. Don't forget that these group plans generally lack the flexibility offered by self-directed plans. Self-directed RESPs that offer the most flexibility are not typically peddled door to door. You've got to take it upon yourself to visit a reputable financial adviser, call a mutual fund company, or contact your bank to set up one of these plans. If a sales person comes knocking, don't commit to anything until you've asked the seven questions I've listed in Tip 39 and you've had a chance to compare with self-directed plans available.

type of investments you can hold in the RESP. Are you happy with the selection? Most mutual fund companies that offer RESPs will offer their own funds and nothing else, but this should not be a problem if their family of funds is diverse. Group plans may not give you a choice in the matter. Are you content with this limitation?

5. *What administrative or other fees apply to the plan, and when?*
- When I set up the plan?
- Each year?
- When withdrawals are made?
- When the plan is terminated?

   Make sure you understand what you're getting into, and how much it's going to cost you. Shop around to find a plan with fees you can stomach. Group plans can be notorious for charging administrative fees when other plans don't. But ask about fees before you eliminate a particular promoter from your short list.

6. *Can I stop making contributions at any time, for as long as I want, without having fees or charges applied?* You'll want the flexibility to control the timing and the amount of the contributions you make to the plan. Most plans will allow complete flexibility here, but check to make sure the plan you're contemplating provides this flexibility.

7. *Can I transfer my RESP assets to another RESP promoter, free of fees or charges?* If you decide later that you'd like to take your RESP money and run—most likely to another promoter—you'll want the opportunity to do so with minimal penalties and fees. Ask your promoter if the plan allows it.

TO MAKE A LONG STORY SHORT:

- Not all RESPs are created equal, and it can be tough to compare one plan to another.

- Ask the promoter seven simple questions before choosing an RESP, to determine just how much flexibility the promoter is able to give you.

Tim's Tip 40: **Choose the subscriber to the RESP carefully.**

Who should be named as the subscriber to an RESP? The person with the money to contribute, right? Not necessarily. For practical reasons, the parents of the beneficiary are the usual subscribers to an RESP. But someone else—grandparents or a doting aunt or uncle— may also be interested in contributing to an RESP.

It's important that all potential subscribers communicate with each other, because the annual contribution limit of $4,000 and the life-time limit of $42,000 is tracked *per beneficiary*, regardless of how many RESPs have been set up for an individual child.

Skye and Randy contributed $3,000 to an RESP this year for their daughter, Chloe. Grandpa Burt contributed $2,000 to another RESP that he has subscribed to with Chloe named as beneficiary. The total contributions for Chloe, then, equalled $5,000 this year. The result? An over-contribution problem (subject to a penalty), since the annual maximum for any beneficiary is just $4,000. The penalty equals 1 percent of the over-contribution ($1,000) for each month-end that it is outstanding.

If the total amount being contributed on behalf of your child exceeds the annual RESP contribution limits, you will need to decide which of the subscribers will use an RESP and which will save money outside the plan. This decision will depend on several factors, including the marginal tax rate of each subscriber. (The person with the highest marginal tax rate will benefit most from the tax-free compounding inside the RESP.)

Finally, if your child decides not to pursue a postsecondary education, it may be possible to transfer the accumulated income in the RESP to the subscriber's RRSP. If the grandparents are the subscribers, there's a good chance they will no longer have an RRSP, since they could be over age 69. Thought should be given, then, to making the parents the subscribers of the plan, even if this means that the grandparents give their contribution to the parents, who then contribute it to the RESP.

TO MAKE A LONG STORY SHORT:

- Where more than one person wants to save for a child's education through an RESP, the subscribers should communicate with each other to make sure the total contributions for the child do not exceed $4,000 annually and $42,000 in the child's lifetime.

- It may be best to have the subscribers in the highest marginal tax bracket contribute to the RESP, and other contributors save outside the RESP.

- Grandparents should consider giving capital to their kids, so the kids can subscribe to an RESP for the grandkids, especially if this arrangement would allow the RESP assets to be rolled over to an RRSP later, if the grandchild decides not to pursue a postsecondary education.

Action Step

When setting up an RESP for your child, consider naming yourself and your spouse (if you have one) as joint subscribers on the plan. This way, if it's necessary to roll RESP assets to an RRSP later, you'll have the choice of which spouse's RRSP to take advantage of. Keep in mind that a "spouse" under our tax law can include someone with whom you've been living in a common-law relationship. In addition, it appears that same-sex couples will soon be considered spouses under our tax law, although at the time of writing, this change to the law had not been made. Check with a tax pro for the current status on this issue.

Tim's Tip 41: **Make sure your RESP is around for at least 10 years.**

One of the highlights of the new RESP rules is that if a child decides not to pursue a postsecondary education, the subscriber to the plan has more options than ever before. I briefly mentioned these options in Tip 35, point 10. You might recall that one of the most attractive options, when none of the beneficiaries of your RESP attends school, is to roll up to $50,000 of the accumulated income of the RESP into your RRSP. Sure, you would need to have sufficient RRSP contribution room to do this, but you would avoid income tax on the accumulated income and the nasty 20 percent penalty that would apply if you took the accumulated income out of the plan for yourself.

Two other requirements must be met if you hope to use this tax-free rollover: (1) the RESP must have been in existence for at least 10 years, and (2) the beneficiaries of the plan must have reached age 21 and not be eligible to receive educational assistance payments (EAPs) from the plan. The rule of thumb is simple: Start an RESP before your child's 11th birthday, to ensure that the plan will have been in existence for at least 10 years by the time your child reaches age 21. In that way, you provide yourself with an opportunity to roll the assets over to your RRSP.

As an aside, you should note that the 10-year and age-21 requirements can be waived if the child is mentally impaired.

TO MAKE A LONG STORY SHORT:

- It's now possible to roll the accumulated income in an RESP over to an RRSP if your child chooses to forgo a college or university education, but only where the plan has existed for 10 years and your child has reached age 21 and is not eligible for educational assistance payments from the plan.

- To ensure you'll qualify for this rollover provision, make sure you set up the RESP by your child's 11th birthday.

Tim's Tip 42: Consider postponing RRSP contributions if it looks like your child won't be enrolling in a postsecondary institution.

There may come a day when you look at your child, contemplate what it is she will be doing in the future, and then conclude that a postsecondary education is not in the cards. At that time, if you've been building up assets in an RESP, you will have to arrive at some sort of plan for those assets. Rolling them over to your RRSP is a great idea, if you have the contribution room.

Here's how it works: As we learned in Tip 41, if your RESP has been around for at least 10 years and the beneficiaries under the plan are all at least age 21 and not pursuing an education, then you can transfer up to $50,000 of your RESP accumulated income to your RRSP. In that year, any accumulated income rolled over to the RRSP will be included in your income as the subscriber, but you'll be entitled to an offsetting deduction for the RRSP contribution you've made. The result? No tax on the assets rolled to the RRSP—and no 20 percent penalty, which would normally apply to accumulated income payments (AIPs) made to a subscriber.

But what if you don't have RRSP contribution room? Here's an idea: In the 5 years leading up to the youngest beneficiary's 21st birthday, consider withholding your normal RRSP contributions if it looks as though you'll need to take advantage of the option to roll your RESP assets over to your RRSP. You would be conserving RRSP contribution room for this purpose. You would be better off taking this approach than not having the RRSP room available and being forced, as the subscriber, to take AIPs. The tax you'll pay on those AIPs could be as high as 70 percent. Think about it: A 50 percent tax if you're in the highest marginal tax bracket, plus a 20 percent penalty, is 70 percent. Yikes! I think I would conserve some RRSP contribution room instead, thanks very much.

TO MAKE A LONG STORY SHORT:

- Rolling RESP assets over to an RRSP can work very well when the beneficiary of an RESP does not go on to a postsecondary education. But you've got to have RRSP contribution room.

- Consider holding off on RRSP contributions in the 5 years leading up to the youngest beneficiary's 21st birthday if it looks like you will need to roll assets from the RESP over to your RRSP. That way, you'd be creating the contribution room you'll need to make the rollover.

Tim's Tip 43: **If your RESP beneficiaries are more than six years apart in age, consider separate plans.**

Picture this. You're the subscriber to an RESP for your three kids, and the oldest of the three is seven years older than the youngest. If you set up the RESP when your first child was just a newborn, you could run into a jam later when your youngest reaches age 18 and enrolls in a qualifying educational program. Consider a hypothetical future scenario featuring my children, Winston and Sarah, and an as yet unborn sibling—let's call him Stephen.

W*inston is going to be 18 years old in a few years. His younger sister Sarah will be 16 at that time, and Stephen will be just 11—7 years younger than Winston. Grandma Margaret and Grandpa Burt set up an RESP for Winston back when he was just a newborn, and they added Sarah and Stephen as beneficiaries when they were born. By the time Stephen reaches age 17 and is almost ready to make withdrawals from the RESP, the plan will have been in existence for 25 years. Since an RESP is only allowed a lifespan of 25 years, the plan will be terminated* *before Stephen can make any withdrawals.*

How do you solve the problem of an RESP terminating before the youngest beneficiary has a chance to take educational assistance payments from the plan? Well, don't bother transferring the remaining assets to a new RESP before the old RESP terminates—it won't work. You see, the new RESP will be deemed to have been created when the old RESP was created. You'll run into the same problem.

The solution is to set up separate RESPs when your children are more than 6 years apart in age. In fact, even when your children are just 4 years apart in age, you may want to consider separate plans if you established the first plan when your oldest child was a newborn. In the example above, the RESP will have to be terminated when Winston is 25 years old. If any of his siblings are age 21 or younger when he reaches age 25, they will likely have a year or two of postsecondary school left, and it would be a shame to have to terminate the RESP while they are still in school. In such a case, the siblings would have to speed up their withdrawals from the plan, which would create more taxable income than necessary in their hands.

Did You Know?

If you properly invest the money inside an RESP, the value of those assets should double every seven to nine years. This is called the "rule of 72." Here's how it works: Divide the number 72 by the after-tax rate of return you're able to earn on your investments, and the result is the approximate number of years that it will take for your money to double. For example, if you're able to generate an 8 percent return on the investments inside the RESP (which should be your minimum goal over the long term), it will take about nine years (72 divided by 8) for the investments to double.

TO MAKE A LONG STORY SHORT:

- An RESP has a lifespan of 25 years maximum.

- When your children are more than six years apart in age, it may be necessary to terminate the RESP before the youngest child reaches postsecondary school—certainly before that child graduates.

- Consider setting up separate plans for children who are more than six years apart in age.

Action Step

I've mentioned on more than one occasion that the investments you set aside for a child's education should be at least 40 percent foreign content. Keep in mind that 40 percent is the minimum. If you had invested $100 in different equity markets back in 1969, the value of that money in 1997 would have been $1,335 (U.S. market), $1,258 (U.K. market), $1,956 (Japanese market), $1,188 (German market), and just $444 in the Canadian market (ignores exchange rate fluctuations). As for my kids, 100 percent of their RESP assets are in foreign content.

Tim's Tip 44: Know your investment options for the RESP.

As part of the draft budget legislation released on October 27, 1998, the government introduced new rules about investments that qualify for RESPs. The rules pretty much mirror the rules for investments that qualify for RRSPs. If we use the RRSP rules as a guide, it's clear that you can hold the following investments in your RESP:

- cash
- shares listed on a prescribed Canadian stock exchange
- shares listed on a prescribed foreign stock exchange
- units of many mutual funds
- shares of Canadian public companie not listed on a prescribed stock exchange

- government or government-guaranteed debt obligations
- corporate bonds or other debt obligations
- GICs
- certain rights or warrants
- other less common investments.

You want to avoid having non-qualifying investments inside your RESP, since they will make you liable for a penalty tax equal to one percent per month of all non-qualifying investments held at the end of each month. Even worse, Revenue Canada has the right to revoke any RESP that holds non-qualifying investments. Both of these provisions became effective January 1, 1999.

In addition to the tax rules, the terms of your RESP might just restrict the types of investments you can hold. For example, a mutual fund company may offer an RESP with the investment choices restricted to their brand of funds only. In most cases this will not be a concern, since the company will undoubtedly offer a large number of funds from which you can choose to achieve an appropriate degree of diversification. An RESP that is fully self-directed (offered by many brokerage firms) presents you with the most flexibility, but the fees may be higher.

Finally, make sure that you hold at least 40 percent of your RESP assets in foreign securities. There is no foreign content limit on RESPs, and in the past, foreign equity markets have outperformed Canadian equity markets over the long term (see Tip 27 in Chapter 3 for more investment ideas).

Don't forget, a group plan doesn't provide you with any control over the investments in your RESP (refer back to Tip 36).

TO MAKE A LONG STORY SHORT:

- Your RESP can hold the same array of investments as your RRSP. Avoid non-qualifying investments because they lead to penalties and can cause your RESP to be revoked.

- Since there are no foreign content limits on an RESP, hold at least 40 percent of your RESP assets as foreign investments, to maximize returns.

Action Step

Your will should be reviewed, and updated if necessary, at least every three years. The next time you review your will, be sure to add a provision that talks about any RESPs that you've set up. It's critical to detail in your will who the subscriber should be in the event of your death, and your wishes for the capital contributed to the plan. Your wishes for the capital should likely be to leave the money in the plan for the use of the beneficiary's education. If the capital is not used for this purpose, a repayment of grants (CESGs) received from the government will be necessary. See Tip 49, point 1.

Tim's Tip 45: **Be sure to designate a successor subscriber in your will.**

You probably don't even want to think about this, but if you're the subscriber to an RESP, your death could leave the RESP in a real bind. Now, I'm not suggesting you're going to leave us in the prime of your life, but think for a minute about who you'd like the subscriber to be in the event of your death. When you subscribe to an RESP and fill out the required forms, there is no provision for you to name a successor. But the question of who should replace you as the subscriber is an important one, since it's the subscriber who is entitled to claim a refund of contributions made to the plan. You certainly wouldn't want the new subscriber to take your money and run. This is particularly true if your intention is to leave the contributed capital in the plan for your child's education.

Here's the bad news: Our tax law, as worded at present, allows any heir of your estate who makes a contribution to the plan after your death to be the new subscriber. So if Uncle Bill or another heir beats, say, your spouse, to it, he could become the next subscriber simply by making a contribution to the plan after your death. Do you really want Uncle Bill to be your successor subscriber? Maybe not.

The new subscriber is entitled to withdraw the capital of the RESP. He will be taxed on any accumulated income payments that come out of the plan, should the beneficiary not attend postsecondary school, and he will assume any other benefits, rights, or obligations that accrue to a subscriber. If you have a specific wish for the capital you've contributed to the RESP—for example, that the beneficiary receive the capital—it would be best to spell this wish out in your will so that the executor and heirs of your estate understand it. See Question 18 in Chapter 8 for more on this issue.

TO MAKE A LONG STORY SHORT:

- Most people haven't given a second thought to who should take over as the subscriber of an RESP on the death of the first subscriber.

- Where more than one person is heir to your estate, the first one to make a contribution to the plan will be the new subscriber, with all the rights and obligations that you currently have—including the right to withdraw the capital of the RESP.

- Name in your will the person you'd like to be the new subscriber, and spell out what you'd like done with the capital contributions in the RESP.

Tim's Tip 46: **Ask for a waiver of penalties if they have been applied.**

It's rare, but from time to time the tax collector will levy penalties on the subscriber of an RESP—usually for making over-contributions to the plan. An over-contribution can happen very easily, without your even recognizing it. Over-contributions are most likely to arise in the following circumstances:

- Two different subscribers name the same child as the beneficiary of an RESP. On a combined basis, they contribute more than $4,000 to the RESPs on behalf of that child. Oops! Looks like a lack of communication.

- The subscriber of an RESP changes the beneficiary of the plan to a new person, who happens to be a beneficiary of another RESP. The contributions made for the former beneficiary are considered by Revenue Canada to have been made for the new beneficiary, dating from when the contributions were originally made. This consideration could result in an over-contribution.

Tori has been the beneficiary of an RESP since her parents, Janice and Peter, set up the plan four years ago. Janice and Peter have contributed the maximum $4,000 each year for Tori over the four years, for total contributions of $16,000. This year, Jack, a friend of the family, decided to name Tori as the beneficiary of his only child's RESP, since this child has decided not to pursue a postsecondary education. Jack had contributed $20,000 over the years to his son's plan. This $20,000 in contributions is now deemed to have been made for Tori, from the day it was contributed to Jack's plan. Since Janice and Peter have already maximized Tori's RESP contributions, the additional contributions from Jack are subject to a penalty as excess contributions. At the rate of 1 percent per month on $20,000, that's a penalty of $2,400 per year on the excess contributions. The penalty applies for 10 years, since it has been 10 years since Jack set up the plan for his son. The total penalty to Jack is $24,000 ($2,400 X 10 years), plus interest on the penalty. Whoa, how's that for a surprise?

The penalties on over-contributions can be steep. The good news? You can ask the government to waive or cancel the penalties. Revenue Canada may waive the amounts where the over-contribution was made as the result of a reasonable error, or where the penalty tax is excessive. Just tell them you're requesting a waiver under subsection 204.91(2) of the *Income Tax Act*.

TO MAKE A LONG STORY SHORT:

- Over-contributions to an RESP can easily happen when two subscribers are contributing to different RESPs for the same beneficiary, or when a beneficiary is named in an RESP in place of a former beneficiary.

- Be sure to ask for a waiver of the penalty when there was a reasonable error, or if the penalty is excessive.

Understanding the New CESG

Many different kinds of grants are available to students today. Research grants are just one type. Here's an interesting story about a researcher. In 1996, backed by $100,000 in U.S. federal, state, and private grants, Kodiak, Alaska, researcher Marion Stirrup developed PlanTea—a nutrient-rich mix of kelp, fish-bone meal, dried beetroot powder, and other ingredients—which she touts as a superior plant food. Stirrup says the list of ingredients came to her telepathically from her 16-inch palm plant, georgiane (which prefers its name spelled with a lower-case G, Stirrup says). Strange, but true.

You don't have to be a plant food researcher—or telepathic—to get the grant I want to talk about here. No sir. All you need to do is make a contribution to an RESP. I'm referring to the Canadian government's Canada Education Savings Grants (CESGs).

Tim's Tip 47: **Understand the basic rules of the CESG.**

RESPs today are more flexible than ever—and they're more popular for this reason. But there's more to RESPs today than new-found flexibility. The big news is the new CESG available to most who contribute to RESPs. It's the CESG that has really turned RESPs into a mainstream savings vehicle. Let's take a closer look at the basic rules around the CESG.

1. *Calculation of the CESG.* The CESG is calculated as 20 percent of any contributions made by a subscriber to an RESP after 1997. The CESG is paid only for beneficiaries who are resident in Canada.

2. *CESG limits.* The maximum grant is $400 for each calendar year. The first $2,000 of contributions in each year will attract the maximum grant ($2,000 X 20% = $400).

3. *Eligible beneficiaries.* A beneficiary is eligible for the CESG up to and including the year in which he reaches age 17. Special rules exist for beneficiaries aged 16 and 17, as follows. To be entitled to the CESG, one of two conditions must be met: either (1) a minimum of $2,000 of RESP contributions has to have been made for the

Did You Know?

If you're looking for more information on the Canada Education Savings Grant, or RESPs in general, you can visit my firm's Web site at www.waterstreet.ca. We've got a discussion forum on the site called "Tax Talk" where you can ask questions and receive free answers from any other participant, many of whom are tax specialists and financial advisers. We've also got a "Mail Bag" area of the site where we post answers to a few questions each week. If this is not enough for you, you'll also find many articles on tax-related issues— including RESPs and CESGs—on the site!

beneficiary before the year in which the beneficiary reaches age 16, or (2) a minimum of $100 in annual RESP contributions has to have been made for the beneficiary in any four years before the year in which the beneficiary reaches age 16. As a transitional measure, a beneficiary who turned 16 or 17 in 1998 will be eligible if he was the beneficiary of an RESP during any four years before 1998.

4. *CESG payments.* The CESG payments are made by the government on a quarterly basis directly to the RESP promoter, who will deposit the amounts in your account when they are received.

5. *CESG room.* Each child is entitled to CESG "room" of $2,000 for each year up to and including the year in which age 17 is reached whether or not an RESP has been set up for the child. Similar to RRSP contribution room, this CESG room is used up as you make contributions to the RESP and claim the grants available. Any grant room not used can be carried forward for use in future years. Once your child is out of CESG room (when the room has been used up through contributions and the claiming of grants), then no further grants are available. (See question 58 in Chapter 8 for more information.)

6. *Excess contributions.* If you make contributions over and above your child's CESG room in one year with the hope of using the excess to receive CESGs in subsequent years, forget it. The rules don't work that way. For example, if your child has CESG room of $2,000, it's not possible to contribute $3,000 to an RESP in the year, use $2,000 of it to receive CESGs in the year, and use the excess $1,000 to receive CESGs in the following year.

7. *Repayment of CESGs.* Situations may arise that could require the repayment of CESGs to the government. I'll talk more about these situations in Tip 49.

Considering Specific CESG Strategies

Tim's Tip 48: Contribute $4,000 to an RESP over every two-year period to maximize CESGs.

You need to understand the workings of the CESG and RESPs. It's easy to get confused. CESG payments are governed by the *Human Resources Development Act (HRDA)*, whereas RESPs, on the other hand, are governed by the *Income Tax Act (ITA)*. This is important to understand because the HRDA will allow you to do certain things that the ITA won't allow you to do. Yes, that's right, they sort of conflict with one another.

Here's what I mean: Under the HRDA, your child is entitled to CESG room of $2,000 each year up to the year she turns 17. The HRDA also allows you to carry forward any unused CESG room. So if you don't make any contributions to an RESP for the next 5 years, your child will accumulate $10,000 of CESG room ($2,000 per year for 5 years). You would think, then, that all you'd need to do at that time is make a $10,000 contribution to your child's RESP, and you'd receive a CESG payment of $2,000 (20 percent of $10,000). In fact, there is nothing in the HRDA to stop you from doing this.

Hold on, though. The ITA won't let you do it. It says the most you can contribute to an RESP in any one year is $4,000. And if you fail to use that contribution room, you can't carry the $4,000 limit forward for use in future years. The bottom line? If your CESG room grows to be significant because you're not making contributions to an RESP, then you may never get to use it all up, since the largest contribution our tax law will allow each year to an RESP is just $4,000.

S*kye and Randy did not open an RESP for Joshua until he was nine years old. Over that nine-year period, Joshua accumulated $18,000 of CESG room, since he's entitled to $2,000 of room each year. At this point, the only way for Joshua to receive* *all the CESG payments for which he is eligible would be for Skye and Randy to contribute $4,000 each year to an RESP until the year Joshua reaches age 17. Take a look at the table below.*

CARRY-FORWARD OF CESG ROOM				
The Calendar Year Child Reaches Age:	Opening CESG Room	Add Current Year CESG Room	Less Current Year Contributions	Closing CESG Room
Newborn	$ –	$ 2,000	$ –	$ 2,000
1	2,000	2,000	–	4,000
2	4,000	2,000	–	6,000
3	6,000	2,000	–	8,000
4	8,000	2,000	–	10,000
5	10,000	2,000	–	12,000
6	12,000	2,000	–	14,000
7	14,000	2,000	–	16,000
8	16,000	2,000	–	18,000
9	18,000	2,000	4,000	16,000
10	16,000	2,000	4,000	14,000
11	14,000	2,000	4,000	12,000
12	12,000	2,000	4,000	10,000
13	10,000	2,000	4,000	8,000
14	8,000	2,000	4,000	6,000
15	6,000	2,000	4,000	4,000
16	4,000	2,000	4,000	2,000
17	2,000	2,000	4,000	–

Here's my rule of thumb: Don't let your child's CESG room grow so large that you'll never be able to claim the CESG payments your child is entitled to receive. Make regular contributions to your RESP. I suggest that you make contributions of $4,000 over every two-year period. Your contribution can be $2,000 each year, or $4,000 every two years. That way, you'll be sure to use up your child's available CESG room as it's created. If you don't do this, you'll be stuck having to make much larger RESP contributions later, as Skye and Randy learned, just to use up the CESG room.

TO MAKE A LONG STORY SHORT:

- Allowing your child's CESG room to build up by failing to make RESP contributions could make it impossible to claim all the CESG payments for which your child is eligible.

- Contribute $4,000 over every two-year period to ensure that you use up the CESG room as it's created.

Tim's Tip 49: **Watch out for the events that could trigger a requirement to repay the CESG.**

For the most part, an RESP can keep the CESG money it receives until the funds are paid out to the beneficiary as part of the educational assistance payments. There are situations, however, that require you to repay the CESGs to the government. The most common is when either contributions or accumulated income are withdrawn for non-educational purposes. In this case, the RESP promoter is required to make a CESG repayment equal to 20 percent of the withdrawal.

Action Step

A sure way to provide yourself with the cash necessary to contribute to an RESP each year is to use your RRSP refund for this purpose. Consider this: A $5,000 RRSP contribution will save you $2,000 in tax if you're the average Canadian. These tax savings typically come back to you as a refund. If you were to contribute that $2,000 refund to an RESP, your eligible child will receive $400 in CESGs. Not only have you boosted the value of the RRSP contribution by another $400, but you now have more money growing tax-sheltered than you had from your RRSP contribution alone.

This rule assumes, of course, that all the contributions to the RESP were "assisted contributions"—that is, they attracted a CESG payment in the first place. Where some contributions were "unassisted," meaning they did not attract a CESG payment (perhaps because they were made before 1998), then assisted contributions will be considered to be withdrawn first, before unassisted contributions. This requirement ensures that the CESGs will be repaid when withdrawals are made for non-educational purposes.

Five situations can give rise to a requirement to repay CESGs:

1. **When contributions are withdrawn for non-educational purposes.** As we discussed earlier, withdrawals of contributions are called "refunds of payments." It's interesting that one of the selling features of RESPs is that the subscriber is able to take back her contributions to the plan. But you should think twice before doing this. If those contributions are withdrawn for non-educational purposes, you can count on repaying some of the CESGs that were received.

2. **When accumulated income is withdrawn for non-educational purposes.** These are the accumulated income payments (AIPs) we talked about earlier. Unless the accumulated income in the plan is paid out for educational purposes as educational assistance payments (EAPs), CESG funds will have to be repaid to the government.

3. **When the plan is terminated or revoked.** The RESP you've set up will automatically terminate at the end of the year in which its 25th anniversary falls. If there is still CESG money in the plan at that time, it will have to be repaid to the government. Likewise, if the RESP were revoked (which could happen if, for example, the plan held non-qualifying investments), the CESG money sitting in the plan at that time would have to be repaid.

4. **When a beneficiary under the plan is replaced.** As a general rule, replacing one beneficiary with another will require you to repay any CESGs that were paid into the RESP on behalf of the former beneficiary. There are two exceptions, however: If the new beneficiary is under age 21 and is either a brother or a sister of the

former beneficiary, or if both the former and the new beneficiaries are related to the subscriber by blood or adoption, then the CESGs do not have to be repaid.

5. **When certain transfers are made from one RESP to another.** The rules say that, when there's a transfer from one RESP to another involving either a change in beneficiaries or a partial transfer of assets, CESG money must be repaid. To avoid this repayment, make sure that the transfer does not involve a change in beneficiaries, and that 100 percent of the assets are transferred from the former RESP to the new plan.

TO MAKE A LONG STORY SHORT:

- CESG money normally stays in the RESP until it's paid out to your child as part of the educational assistance payments.

- CESGs must be repaid in five situations: (1) when contributions are withdrawn for non-educational purposes, (2) when the accumulated income in the plan is withdrawn for non-educational purposes, (3) when the plan is terminated or revoked, (4) when a beneficiary under a plan is replaced (with some exceptions), and (5) when certain transfers are made from one RESP to another.

Tim's Tip 50: Leave your unassisted contributions in the plan.

When I hear the word "unassisted," I automatically think of Mario Lemieux. He was probably professional hockey's purest goal scorer before he retired a few years ago. Fans in Pittsburgh were accustomed to hearing the announcement: "Goal scored by number 66, Mario Lemieux, *unassisted*. Time of the goal: 19:30."

My brother-in-law Ned isn't Mario Lemieux on the ice (believe me, I can vouch for that), but he's definitely the king of "unassisted contributions." Unassisted contributions to an RESP are simply contributions made to the plan for which no CESG payments were received. For example, any contributions made before 1998 are considered unassisted contributions because CESGs were not around back then. Today, you could make an unassisted contribution if there is no more CESG contribution room available to your child but you make a contribution to the RESP anyway.

The Potential Abuse

The tax collector has recognized that there's a potential for RESP subscribers to abuse unassisted contributions. Here's what I mean: If you were to withdraw all the unassisted contributions that you made to your RESP before 1998 (before the CESG was around) and re-contributed those funds to another RESP, you might expect to receive CESG payments on those funds this time around. You would, in effect, be recycling those RESP contributions to get the government grants. Not so fast! The tax collector has come up with a plan to prevent this type of recycling of contributions.

The Rules

You have to understand the implications of withdrawing unassisted contributions from an RESP. Any time after February 23, 1998, that you make a withdrawal of unassisted contributions from an RESP for non-educational purposes, you'll face restrictions on future CESG payments for the beneficiaries of that plan.

If you take the time to read through the frequently asked questions and answers on RESPs and CESGs that I've listed in Chapter 8, you'll quickly discover one very important rule of thumb: When transferring assets from one RESP to another, you should always be sure to transfer 100 percent of the assets. Transferring just a portion of the assets can lead to problems. Most notably, you may have to repay any CESGs received, and your child might suffer a loss of some CESG room because of the "unassisted contribution" rules that I've talked about in Tip 50.

Caution!

These restrictions also apply if you transfer, after February 23, 1998, any unassisted contributions from one RESP to another.

The restrictions look like this: Any contributions made to any RESP during the remainder of the year of the withdrawal, or in the following two years, on behalf of those beneficiaries will not be eligible for the CESG. And there's more. The beneficiaries of that RESP will not earn new CESG room for those two following years. These restrictions won't apply where the total withdrawals of unassisted contributions in the year amount to $200 or less, or where there's a full transfer of assets from one RESP to another and no change in beneficiaries.

TO MAKE A LONG STORY SHORT:

- Unassisted contributions to an RESP are those contributions that did not give rise to any CESG payment from the government.

- The potential exists for wily subscribers to abuse unassisted contributions by recycling them to receive CESGs, so the tax collector introduced rules to prevent this situation from happening.

- The bottom line: Your child will lose some CESGs and CESG room if you make a withdrawal of unassisted contributions from an RESP—with minor exceptions.

Tim's Tip 51: **Spread out your RESP contributions to maximize the CESGs if necessary.**

You may recall that it's not possible to make excess contributions in one year with the hope of carrying them forward and claiming a CESG in a subsequent year. I talked about this in Tip 47, point 6. Let me give you an example.

*J*anice and Peter are joint subscribers of an RESP for their son
Lincoln. This year, they contributed $4,000 to his RESP, but
they don't expect to make any contributions next year. Since
Lincoln has $3,000 of CESG room available ($2,000 for this year
plus $1,000 carried forward from a prior year), they received a
$600 grant on the first $3,000 contributed to the plan this year.
They were not entitled to receive CESG payments on the excess
$1,000 contributed this year. Nor can they "allocate" that excess
$1,000 to next year to claim CESG payments on it then.

Here's a potential dilemma: If you're able to make contributions
this year to an RESP that exceed your child's CESG room, but you
don't expect to make any contributions next year, you'd be better off
spreading the contributions over two years. Go back to my example
above. Janice and Peter received no grants on the excess $1,000 they
contributed to Lincoln's RESP this year. They don't plan to make any
contributions next year, so they won't receive any CESG payments
next year. They would have been better off to have split the $4,000
contribution in two, contributing $3,000 this year and $1,000 next
year. By doing so, they would have received a $600 CESG this year
and another $200 CESG next year.

The rule is simple: Consider spreading your RESP contributions
over more than one year if it means you'll be entitled to more CESG
payments. The only disadvantage, of course, to delaying a contribution to an RESP is that you won't be taking advantage of the tax-free
compounding inside the RESP as soon as you could. But if you're
talking about delaying the contribution by just one year, and this
delay creates more CESG payments for your child, chances are pretty
good you'll be better off taking my advice and spreading the contributions over the two years.

TO MAKE A LONG STORY SHORT:

- You won't receive CESG payments for contributions to an RESP in excess of your child's CESG room each year.

- Consider splitting the contributions over more than one year if it means receiving more in CESG payments.

WINNING THE EDUCATION SAVINGS GAME

If you knew nothing about RESPs and CESGs before reading this chapter, your head might just be spinning by now. There's a lot to know! Take the time to digest the information, and if need be, go back and review Tip 35 for the basics on RESPs, and Tip 47 for the basics on CESGs. For those of you who have a good grasp of this stuff already and are looking for answers to more difficult questions about these plans, I've designed Chapter 8 just for you. In any event, it's important to understand RESPs and CESGs if you hope to win the education savings game. After all, as you've learned by now, an RESP should form the cornerstone of any properly planned education savings program. Now, refer to the Education Planning Tip Sheet at the front of the book and put a check mark next to those tips that you want to make note of.

THE HONOUR ROLL: OTHER FUNDING STRATEGIES

When we deliberate it is about means and not ends.

—Aristotle

6

I can think of no more worthwhile cause for which to beg, borrow, steal, sweat, and save than obtaining a college or university education. The cost of a postsecondary education is high—no question—but it has become increasingly important, and will remain so as we move into the future. Aside from the long-term financial benefits of a postsecondary education, the life experiences acquired along with that education will shape the perspectives and potential of tomorrow's leaders.

Consider, for example, the experience of a group of students from Harvey Mudd College in Claremont, California. In 1996, the *Los Angeles Times* reported on a pioneering class project at the college, in which students aimed to develop an alternative, manure-based fuel supply for Guatemalans in a village where firewood is scarce. In order to produce realistic, village-based waste, one student was designated to eat only beans, rice, and tortillas for a week. The diet, however, made him constipated, and the project was scrapped when it couldn't be completed by the due date.

How, you're wondering, did this experience shape the lives of the students who participated? Well, it gave them an appreciation for the plight of Guatemalan villagers and a new understanding of the effects of Central American food on the North American human digestive system.

Alright, it's a bad example. But it's a good story—and a true one at that. My point is, an education is worth having—at almost any cost.

Now that I've talked at length about RESPs, I want to tell you that the RESP is just one of the tools—albeit a very important one—available to save for education. Because I want to provide you with as many tools as I can, let me introduce seven alternative funding strategies for you to consider.

These other strategies can also be categorized as begging, borrowing, stealing, sweating, and saving. I've got a strategy for you in each category—in fact, three under "saving." It's unlikely you'll be able to take advantage of all these strategies, but you should be aware they exist—just in case.

Making Use of Trusts

Tim's Tip 52: Make use of an in-trust account when an RESP won't be enough.

This one's a savings strategy. An in-trust account is really nothing more than an investment or bank account opened for your child. The money in the account usually comes from a parent or other related adult, and an adult's name is usually on the account along with the child's name. In-trust accounts have been the most popular method of saving for a child's education over the last few years. Why? Because RESPs were downright ugly as a savings vehicle until the federal government performed radical surgery on them in 1997 and 1998.

Even with the new RESP in place, an in-trust account can still be an effective method of saving for your child's education, particularly when you don't have a lot of time to save and it's unlikely that you'll be able to sock away enough in an RESP because of the $4,000 annual contribution limit. There are no limits as to how much you can invest in an in-trust account.

Income Splitting

The real reason for setting up an in-trust account is to facilitate income splitting with your child. Here's how it works: If you contribute money to an in-trust account for your minor child, any capital gains earned on the account will be taxed in the child's hands, not yours. And if your child has little or no other income, chances are he won't pay any tax. You'd be smart to avoid earning interest and dividends in the account, since the tax bill on those forms of income will be passed back to you under the "attribution rules" in our tax law.

Action Step

Capital gains realized on the investments in an in-trust account will generally be taxed in the hands of the child. Since the child is likely to have little or no other income, there is generally little or no tax to pay when gains are realized. Further, it's a good idea to sell the profitable investments and reinvest the proceeds every few years. Why? Because this is not likely to result in a tax bill to the child, but will increase the adjusted cost base (ACB) of the investments to the fair market value at the selling date. A higher ACB will mean lower taxable gains later.

Potential Problems

If you don't set up the in-trust account properly, you might just shoot yourself in the foot. You see, if certain conditions aren't met, the tax collector might tax *you*—the contributor—on all the income in the account, including the capital gains—which would defeat the purpose of setting up the account in the first place.

To avoid this problem, Revenue Canada wants some assurance that you have "divested, deprived, or dispossessed" yourself of the funds you transferred to your child—that is, that the funds now truly belong to the child, not you. What you do with the money you've transferred to the in-trust account will speak volumes about whether or not you've truly passed ownership to your child. You can't, for example, take the money back and use it for that home renovation project or that tropical vacation.

And there's more. Subsection 75(2) of the *Income Tax Act* will still tax you on all the income in the account unless you ensure that

- you are not the contributor to the account and the trustee at the same time
- you name the beneficiaries of the account up front
- the property in the account never reverts back to you.

When I set up an in-trust account for my son, Winston, I made my wife, Carolyn, trustee. The name on the account reads "Carolyn Cestnick, in trust for Winston Cestnick." This way, I'm not both the contributor and the trustee. If I were, I'd have a problem under subsection 75(2) of our tax law, and I'd be the one to pay all the tax on the account. Notice that I named Winston as the beneficiary. This was critical. If I had simply named the account "Carolyn Cestnick in trust," without naming a beneficiary, I'd run into problems under 75(2) again. Finally, I'm going to make sure the assets in the account stay there. They will never revert to me. If they did, 75(2) would catch me again.

A Trust By Any Other Name

Many lawyers are of the opinion that an in-trust account is really a "bare" trust (even though it has nothing to do with being naked!). Provincial trust law says that, under a bare trust, the trustee has no authority other than to hold the assets for the beneficiary until the beneficiary asks for the assets, which he can do once he reaches the age of majority. Yes, your child has the right to use the assets in the account for any purpose once he reaches the age of majority, and an education may not be the first thing that comes to his mind.

Let me make one last point. Some people argue that an in-trust account is not truly a legal trust. If they are right, then you'll avoid the problems under subsection 75(2) of the *Income Tax Act* that I spoke about earlier, and you won't have to worry about provincial trust law handing your child the assets at age of majority. To allow a proper splitting of income, however, Revenue Canada still wants assurances that the assets truly belong to the child. And that means leaving the assets in the account for your child, not using them for your own benefit.

TO MAKE A LONG STORY SHORT:

- An in-trust account should be considered whenever you won't be able to save enough through an RESP alone—for example, when you don't have much time to save for your child's education.

- Make sure you meet the three conditions that avoid problems with Revenue Canada: (1) the contributor should not also be the trustee, (2) a beneficiary should be named, and (3) the assets should never revert back to the contributor.

Tim's Tip 53: **Consider a family trust when you want complete flexibility in controlling the assets that are being set aside.**

Here's another savings strategy. A trust is simply a legal arrangement between three parties: the settlor (who transfers assets to the trust), the trustee (who holds title to the assets), and the beneficiary (the person for whom the assets are held). A trust created during your lifetime is called an *inter vivos* trust. When you hear the term "family" trust, it most commonly refers to a formal *inter vivos* trust, with usually parents (or grandparents) as settlors and their children (or grandchildren) as beneficiaries.

A family trust is different from an in-trust account in that a family trust involves a formal trust agreement, which provides for the types of investments that can be held in the trust, the powers of the trustees, and other matters.

A family trust offers the ultimate flexibility over the investment options available, the timing of payouts to beneficiaries, and the use of funds in the trust. Let's take a closer look at these benefits.

A family trust can hold assets of any type, as long as the trust agreement permits, including, among other things, cash, stocks, bonds, mutual funds, real estate, and shares in a private company. If the purpose of the family trust is to save for your child's education, some investments will be more appropriate than others. For example, real estate may not be a good choice since it's not very liquid and it's higher risk than blue-chip equity investments.

Next, you can't beat the flexibility in the timing of payouts to the kids that is offered by a family trust. Unlike an RESP (which requires your child to enroll in a postsecondary school and terminates after 25 years) or an in-trust account (which hands the assets over to the child when she reaches the age of majority), a family trust allows you to specify exactly when the assets in the trust will be paid out to your children and under what conditions.

Finally, a family trust will not bind you to using the assets for any particular purpose, unless you prefer that it do so. The trust agreement will allow you to do whatever you like in this regard.

You can also use the family trust for income splitting—much like the in-trust account I spoke about in Tip 52. Any income in the trust that is paid or payable to the beneficiaries will be taxed in their hands provided they are 18 or over. For minors, interest and dividends will be taxed in the settlor's hands under the attribution rules (except for second-generation income—that is, income on income—which is not attributed back). Capital gains, however, will not be attributed to you. They will be taxed in the hands of the beneficiaries if the amounts are paid or payable to them.

The 1999 federal budget made some changes to income splitting arrangements through family trusts where the trust receives dividends or business income from a family business. In this case, where the income is passed to the hands of minor children to be taxed, it will be taxed at the highest marginal rate going.

There's no doubt that a formal family trust is going to cost more to set up and maintain on an annual basis than an RESP or an in-trust account. And you're going to need the help of a lawyer to set up a formal trust. For these reasons, family trusts are most useful for those who can set aside close to $100,000 in the trust over a five-year period or so. If you're not in this position, one of the other education savings options is probably better for you.

TO MAKE A LONG STORY SHORT:

- A family trust is a formal *inter vivos* trust that offers more flexibility than RESPs and in-trust accounts when it comes to investments, timing of payouts, and use of the funds in the trust.

- Formal trusts cost much more to set up and administer than simple in-trust accounts, and are most appropriate when assets of about $100,000 will make their way to the trust over a relatively short period.

Insuring Your Child's Future

Tim's Tip 54: Life insurance can work as a savings vehicle, but only if the conditions are right.

Now for the third savings strategy. It may seem like a strange idea, but buying insurance on the life of your child could provide a way to save for her education. You see, a universal life insurance policy has one very special characteristic: You can invest money inside the policy and watch it grow on a tax-sheltered basis, much like it would inside an RRSP. If you start when your child is very young, a decent education fund can build up inside the policy by the time she is ready to hit the books.

Here's how it works. Every dollar in premiums you pay is split into two parts. The first part is used to pay for the insurance on your child's life, while the second part is added to the growing pool of investments in the policy. At some point (usually when your child reaches age 18), you can transfer ownership of the policy to your child on a tax-free basis. She can then make withdrawals of the accumulated investments to pay for her studies at college or university. She will have to pay some tax on these withdrawals, but because she's likely to have little or no other income, the tax hit will probably be minimal.

Most universal life policies have a decent selection of investments to choose from. Quite often these investments include fixed-income accounts, guaranteed-interest accounts, and index-linked accounts (typically linked to a stock index). The result? The investment component to the policy can grow at a respectable rate.

Unlike an RESP, a life insurance policy does not have contribution limits, provided the child is insurable. Further, there are no restrictions on when or how the money should be used. Keep in mind, however, that this strategy can be expensive, since you're paying for life insurance on a child, and it's life insurance you probably will not need. Still, check out the numbers.

The figures in the table on the following page come courtesy of my friends at Pan Financial in Toronto. Allow me to interpret these numbers for you. There are two investment accounts shown in this table.

The first is a regular investment account (an in-trust account, for example), and the second is the investment component to a universal life insurance policy. In both cases, a deposit of $2,750 is made each year. By the end of the year in which the child turns age 5, the regular investment account has a balance of $16,145 and is ahead of the life insurance policy, which has an investment component of $13,864. By the end of year in which the child reaches age 18, the regular account amounts to $84,652 while the investments in the life insurance policy amount to $90,447—slightly ahead of the regular account.

In this example, the student will be able to make withdrawals from the regular investment account of $25,000 for the first three

Don't automatically assume that a life insurance policy is best as a savings plan just because the numbers look good. The numbers can look completely different when you change the assumptions about tax rates and rates of return. In addition, you've got to realize that withdrawals from the regular account are generally tax-free since the funds represent tax-paid money, while a portion of the withdrawals from the insurance policy are likely taxable. You've got to look at the money in the student's hands after taxes.

Caution!

		Balance End of Year	
Age of Child	**Withdrawal From Investments**	**Regular Investment Account**	**Investment Component of Insurance Policy**
1		$ 2,899	$ 2,300
5		16,145	13,864
10		37,145	34,597
15		64,462	65,562
18		84,652	90,447
19	$ 25,000	62,873	72,012
20	25,000	39,919	52,353
21	25,000	15,724	31,263
22	25,000	–	8,582

LIFE INSURANCE FOR EDUCATION SAVINGS

Assumptions:
1. Rate of return on regular investment account is 9% annually.
2. Tax rate on taxable account is 40%.
3. Rate of return on investment component of insurance policy is 7.9% annually.
4. Annual deposit amounts of $2,750 are made for 18 years to both regular investment account and life insurance policy.

years. In the fourth year of school (at age 22), there will only be $15,724 for the student to withdraw. With the insurance policy, the student will be able to make withdrawals of $25,000 every year for four years, and will still be left with $8,582 at the end of the fourth year. Is the insurance option really the better choice here? Not necessarily. The figures don't show how much tax will be owing by your child on the payments from each account.

In short, the two accounts may be more equal than the numbers appear, depending on the assumptions you make. Before choosing the life insurance option, ask a life insurance broker to run the numbers for you using a variety of assumptions. Ask what portion of the withdrawals will be taxable once the withdrawals are made from the life insurance by the child.

TO MAKE A LONG STORY SHORT:

- A universal life insurance policy has an investment component that grows on a tax-sheltered basis and that can be used as an education fund.

- Your child will have to pay some, but likely little, tax when she makes withdrawals for her education.

- The strategy could be expensive, since you're paying for life insurance on a child, which is insurance you probably don't need.

Asking Your Employer For Help

Tim's Tip 55: **If you're already in the workforce, ask your employer to contribute to your education.**

This is a begging strategy, to be considered if your children are already in the workforce—or for you, if you're looking to upgrade your education.

I've always said that Canadian employers are thoroughly uncreative when it comes to compensating their employees. A salary increase may be a generous gesture from the boss, but after Revenue Canada takes its share, it may be just half the gesture it was intended to be. Enter non-taxable benefits. Your employer can pay for certain things that will be considered tax-free benefits to you. And tax-free benefits are the best kind—after all, they never show up on your T4 slip.

Education costs are one of those benefits that you can receive tax-free. Now, Revenue Canada's policy on these benefits changed in 1998. The tax collector has clarified that there are three types of education costs. Two are tax-free, but the third is taxable. Here they are:

Specific Employment-Related Training

Any courses you take to maintain or upgrade employer-related skills—that is, skills directly related to your work—are not taxable benefits when they're paid for by your employer. For example, if you're a printer and your boss sends you on a course to learn about a new printing press, that benefit is not taxable. The key here is that your employer expects to benefit from your education, so you're sheltered from the tax collector.

General Employment-Related Training

Say your employer is willing to pay for courses that are not directly related to your work, but they are generally related to it. I'm talking about courses like stress management, employment equity, and other general programs. These course will typically be tax-free.

Personal Interest Training

What if you were hoping your boss would pay for those flight lessons or that furniture recovering course? If he does, you can expect it to be a taxable benefit (unless you're in the business of flying or recovering furniture, of course). These are personal interest courses, and you're the primary person who'll benefit—not your employer.

TO MAKE A LONG STORY SHORT:

- Education costs paid for by your employer can be a tax-free benefit to you.

- Personal interest courses paid for by your employer, however, are taxed in your hands. They'll show up on your T4 slip.

Utilizing the Family Business

Tim's Tip 56: **Lend money to your adult child through a corporation if you're a business owner.**

Here's a clever little borrowing strategy that can work wonders if you're a business owner and you'd like to use some of the cash in your corporation to help finance your child's education.

The strategy involves your corporation making a loan to your child. This loan will be included in your child's income under subsection 15(2) of our tax law. The good news? Your child will likely pay little or no tax on the loan if he has little or no other income. But the story doesn't end here. Once your child has graduated from school and is working full-time, he can repay the loan to the company. At that time, he will be entitled to a deduction for the repayment under paragraph 20(1)(j) of the tax law.

Did you catch those benefits? Your child pays little or no tax when receiving the cash, *and* receives a deduction for repaying the loan at a time when his income is much higher, due to full-time employment, and deductions are welcome.

Action Step

The 1999 federal budget proposed changes to our tax law that will prevent your corporation from making loans for education (or anything else for that matter) to a minor child related to you. If the child is a minor, the loan will be taxable to the child, but at the highest marginal tax rate going. The result? A tax bill of about 50 percent in the child's hands. For this reason, make sure that any corporate loan to your child is made only after the child has reached age 18.

When our daughter Sarah reaches age 18, we will provide her with a $10,000 loan from our family corporation for her schooling. Assuming she has no other income at that time, she won't pay any tax on that loan, after taking into consideration her basic personal credit and the tuition and education credits she can expect to receive. When she graduates from school, she will repay the loan. Each repayment will be deductible on her tax return. Even at the lowest marginal tax rate, she'll save 26 cents in tax for each dollar she repays, thanks to the deduction. Not a bad deal for Sarah! Tax-free cash for school, and a tax deduction when the loan's repaid.

Keep in mind that because this is a loan, it's not deductible by the corporation. You'll also have to be prepared for the fact that your child may be slow to pay back the loan—if he repays it at all! (But I'll leave you to work out the details with your kid yourself.)

TO MAKE A LONG STORY SHORT:

- If you're a business owner and you operate through a corporation, it's possible to make a loan from the company to your adult child for school (or for any purpose, for that matter).

- The loan will be taxable in your child's hands, but will attract little or no tax if he has little or no income. He will also be able to deduct the repayments he makes after graduation, which will save him tax at a time when he is earning an income.

Tim's Tip 57: Pay your child to work in the family business to provide a source of education funding.

Finally, the sweating strategy. This is one of the tried, tested, and true ways to put cash into your child's hands on a tax-efficient basis. Of course, it does require that you have a business of some kind.

Provided your child is working in the business in some way, you'll be able to pay her a reasonable salary or wage. If, for example, you pay your child $6,000 to work in your business in the summer, your business will be entitled to claim a deduction for her wages and she will report the $6,000 as income. If your child has little or no other income, the tax on that $6,000 will be small or non-existent. Your child can then use the money earned to help pay for her education (or for a stereo, CDs, and a Mexican vacation, for that matter).

There's more. Your child will have created RRSP contribution room thanks to this earned income. This contribution room will save her tax down the road when she makes contributions to an RRSP—

most likely after graduation. (Of course, contributions can be made at any time. It's wise, however, to save RRSP deductions for a year when income is higher.)

TO MAKE A LONG STORY SHORT:

- You can pay a reasonable salary or wages to a child who works in your business to help pay for her education.

- This strategy generates a deduction for your business, but it's not likely to result in much tax for your child.

- Your child will also receive valuable RRSP contribution room as a result of earning this money.

Opting to Use RRSP Assets

Tim's Tip 58: Consider using your RRSP assets to fund an education for yourself or your spouse.

Here's the stealing strategy. The 1998 federal budget introduced a new program called the Life Long Learning plan. It allows Canadians to make withdrawals from their RRSPs to pay for an education. I know, I know—this isn't going to help your 18-year-old very much because she doesn't have an RRSP. True enough. This program, however, could help

Did You Know?

It pays to make repayment to your RRSP as quickly as possible after you've withdrawn money under the Life Long Learning plan. In fact, if you were to borrow $20,000 from your RRSP under the program and pay back the funds over a five-year period instead of a ten-year period, you'd end up with $12,840 more in your RRSP after 20 years, assuming an 8 percent rate of return annually.

those who are pursuing an education at a somewhat older age than your traditional student. The plan became effective in 1999 and works much like the plan that allows you to withdraw funds from your RRSP to buy a home.

Withdrawing Funds

You can make tax-free withdrawals from your RRSP of up to $10,000 each year over a four-year period, to a maximum of $20,000 in total, to pay for your full-time education or that of your spouse. You'll be glad to know that you don't have to enroll in a four-year program to qualify. A "full-time" qualifying program can be as short as three months. And if you're disabled, your attendance can be on a part-time basis.

Repaying the Money

You'll have to repay those tax-free withdrawals you made from your RRSP over a 10-year period. Your first payment must be made no later than the first 60 days of the 6th year after your first withdrawal. So if you make a withdrawal in 2000, your first payment will be due in the first 60 days of 2006. In certain situations, you have to start your repayments sooner.

Making the Decision (Is This Really a Good Idea?)

If you've been paying attention, you know by now that I normally discourage people from taking money out of their RRSPs for any reason, but particularly if their savings are not yet sufficient to provide a secure retirement. But if your retirement needs can still be met through the timely repayment of funds borrowed from your RRSP for an education, then the idea can make sense. You'll give up some growth inside your RRSP for sure when those assets are withdrawn. You may want a financial adviser to calculate for you how much growth you'll lose. Compare this to the additional income you're likely to earn from the education you receive to see if you can really expect to come out ahead.

TO MAKE A LONG STORY SHORT:

• Under the federal government's Life Long Learning plan, it's possible to make tax-free withdrawals from your RRSP for your education or that of your spouse.

• The most you can withdraw is $20,000 over four years, and you'll have to repay the amount borrowed over a 10-year period once you've finished school.

• This plan makes most sense when withdrawing the assets from your RRSP will not hurt your retirement security.

WINNING THE EDUCATION SAVINGS GAME

I've devoted this chapter to looking at some alternative strategies to help pay for your child's education. Some of the ideas apply to business owners, while others can be used by everyone. In any case, it's good to have a full complement of tools in your tool box to help pay for your child's education. The most popular of the strategies I've presented in this chapter is the in-trust account, and it works well if an RESP won't be enough. Take the time now to visit the Education Planning Tip Sheet at the front of the book and note which tips you'd like to follow up with further action.

THE STUDY OF MONEY: FINANCIAL PLANNING FOR STUDENTS

When I was eighteen, I wanted to save the world. Now, I'd be happy to save a hundred dollars.
—Earl Wilson

7

I was teaching a group of grade 8 students not long ago about money management, entrepreneurship, and economics. It was a fun class, but I sensed that not all the kids got the hang of money management. Near the end of the course, one of the boys approached me and explained with pride how he had managed to make some money.

"How much did you make?" I asked.

"A th-thousand bucks," he stammered excitedly.

"That's great!" I said. "Why don't you tell the class how you did it?"

He stood in front of his classmates and told his story. "Last week I went down to the variety store and stole a chocolate bar. I went home, called Crime Stoppers, and turned myself in. I made a thousand bucks!"

Not exactly what I had in mind when I encouraged the kids to be creative in their money-making.

If your child is like most, he's going to learn a lot about money management by watching you. Heaven knows, they don't teach this stuff in school (my class was an exception)! If you don't want your child to pick up your bad habits, you should take steps to teach him how to manage money properly and how he can help implement the financial planning strategies in this chapter that apply to your family's situation.

The purpose of this chapter is simply to share some general financial planning strategies that will help your child—and you—keep more of your hard-earned money. Financial planning can be broken down into a number of different areas including cash management, debt management, tax, retirement, investment, insurance, and estate planning. In this chapter, let's focus on the four areas that any student should be concerned about:

- cash management
- debt management
- tax planning
- investment planning

Managing Cash Flow

Cash is king. If your child can't manage her cash flow, nothing else in her financial planning will matter much. So a brief talk about cash management is first on the list of priorities here.

If your children are still young, take the time to teach them proper money management habits. It's easy to do. Start by giving your child an allowance at about age eight. Make sure that your child takes a portion of his allowance (10 percent is good) and places it in a savings account for the future—perhaps for a major purchase. This will teach the importance of saving. Encourage your child to think carefully about how he'll use the balance of his allowance, and not to spend all of it impulsively.

Tim's Tip 59: Monitor your child's spending habits and step in when signs of danger appear.

If your child's outflow is greater than his income, then his upkeep will be his downfall. Put simply, your child should make sure he is spending less than he earns. It's not Rocket Science 101, but it's a foolproof formula. And it's a formula that's even more important to adhere to when your child is not earning much money.

For many students, bad spending habits are made worse during those months when they're working full-time and finally have income available. Make sure that, during those work periods, your child sets aside the money you expect him to contribute to his own education (the sweating component of your child's education plan). A separate bank account for these funds makes a lot of sense. It will be one big worry off your mind—and your child's mind—if he does a good job at setting money aside for school as he earns it.

Even if your child manages to save some money for school, he can still get himself into a financial bind if he isn't careful about how much he's spending throughout the school year—even after his tuition has been paid for. Watch for these signs that your child could be living beyond his means:

• He borrows more money from you than you expected.

- He borrows money from friends.
- He works so many hours that it could jeopardize his marks in school.
- He regularly misses the minimum payment on his credit card.
- He applies for more than one credit card.
- He receives frequent statements from the same creditors.
- He receives phone calls from creditors looking for payment.
- He orders pizza three nights in a row and gives a bigger tip to the delivery guy each time.
- He buys you Giorgio Armani underwear for your birthday.

Okay, you can skip the last two—he may just be developing a generous spirit. But if you suspect that your child is not managing his cash flow well, it's time to speak with him about it. Explain that a bad credit rating could jeopardize his financial future by making it difficult to borrow for important things (like a home, car, business or investments). Further, make it clear that you have decided not to bail him out if he manages his money irresponsibly.

TO MAKE A LONG STORY SHORT:

- Your child should be spending less than he's earning. Bad spending habits are often magnified during the months when your child is working full-time.

- Make sure your child sets aside money for school after each paycheque when he's working full-time.

- Watch for the signs that your child is in financial trouble, and intervene if you see this happening.

Reducing the Burden of Debt

Debt is a lot like electricity. Electricity can be extremely useful, and even necessary, but if your child sticks her finger in the socket, she can hurt herself. When debt is used prudently, it can help your child pay for that education that is so important. When debt is abused, it can scar her financially for years to come. Refer back to Tips 18, 19, and 32 for more on student debt, including the limits your child should adhere to when borrowing for school.

Tim's Tip 60: **Manage student debt properly to minimize the interest costs and maintain a good credit rating.**

You'll recall from our talk in Tip 15 way back in Chapter 3 that the level of student debt is on the rise. Chances are pretty good that your child will graduate with up to $20,000 or more of debt. How should he manage this debt? Should the debt be paid off as soon as possible? Which debt is most important to pay off—credit cards, car loans, or student loans? Good questions. Let's look at the answers.

In general, being debt-free is the ideal. This means that paying off debt—including student loans—should be a priority. But which loans should be paid off first? The most expensive debt, of course. I'm talking about debt that carries a high interest rate, and at the same time is not deductible for tax purposes. More than likely, this will be credit card debt. Then, if your child has taken out a loan for a non-deductible purpose (a car loan is probably not deductible unless your child is required to use the car for business or employment), that loan should be next on the hit list.

Student loans, as I mentioned in Tip 18, now come with tax relief. A student will be able to claim a tax credit for any interest paid after 1997 on student loans. As a result, it probably makes the most sense for your child to pay off his student loans after he's paid off his non-deductible debt. That is, if your child is going to extend any loan to 5 or 10 years, it should probably be his student loans, given the tax relief that applies to the interest on this loan.

If your child has other debt that is deductible for tax purposes (for example, a loan for an investment or business), it should be paid off last—even after student loans. Why? Because you get a tax credit for the interest costs on a student loan, whereas you get a tax *deduction* for the interest on a truly "deductible" loan. My book *Winning the Tax Game* covers the differences between a tax deduction and a tax credit more thoroughly. Suffice it to say here that you'll generally save more tax dollars with an interest deduction than with a credit.

To recap, students should pay their debt in the following order:

- non-deductible debt with a high interest rate
- non-deductible debt with a lower interest rate
- student loans (because of the interest credit)
- other, deductible debt.

I'd like to make one comment here about credit card debt. If your child should understand anything about credit cards, it's this: Nothing is more detrimental to his credit rating (to anybody's credit rating!) than being late with a credit card payment—even a day late. Every time a credit card payment is made late, a note is made in the person's credit history. Three strikes and your child might find that borrowing money becomes a very difficult task. All your child needs to do is pay the minimum amount shown on the card's statement *on time*. That's it. Make sure your child understands this—and set a good example yourself.

Action Step

Many students, like their parents, quickly pick up bad credit card habits. It's not unusual to find students who have applied for special student credit cards (available with no credit history, but with a limit of just $500) and have run the cards to their limit. If credit card misuse becomes a problem during school, or after, recommend this idea to your child: The credit card can be placed in a glass of water and stored in the freezer. This is not as effective as cutting up the card, but it will force your child to think twice before using it.

TO MAKE A LONG STORY SHORT:

- Managing debt is a matter of paying off the debt as soon as possible.

- The most expensive non-deductible loans should be paid off first (credit card debt, usually), followed by other non-deductible debt, student loans, and then deductible debt last.

Planning for Tax Savings

You may wonder why your child should be thinking about tax planning when she's not earning much money. The tax bill I'm hoping to reduce here is not your child's current one. After all, your child is not likely to be paying much tax at the moment. The ideas I'm going to share with you will help to reduce your child's future taxes, and your own taxes today.

One of the strategies I'll be introducing in Tip 63 involves splitting income with your child. Splitting income is the process of moving income from the hands of one family member who will pay tax at a higher rate, to the hands of another who will pay tax at a lower rate. But we've got to be careful of the attribution rules here. You might recall that the attribution rules are those rules in our tax law that will cause any interest or dividends earned by your minor child to be taxed in *your* hands, not your child's hands, when you've given her money. But there are ways around the attribution rules. (Hey, I'm a tax specialist; I know these things.) We'll look at three alternatives in Tip 63.

Tim's Tip 61: **Take maximum advantage of all tax credits available to students.**

Students are given special tax breaks by the tax collector. Some come in the form of tax credits. In case you're wondering, a tax credit is an

Keep in mind that your child will need form T2202A, Tuition and Education Amount Certificate, to support any tuition credit claim. This certificate is issued by the school. If your child has been attending a foreign school, then form TL11A, Tuition Fees Certificate (University Outside Canada), must be completed and signed by an authority at the foreign school. You or your child will have to complete the back of form T2202A to determine how much of the credits can be transferred to you.

amount that reduces a tax bill dollar for dollar. It differs from a tax deduction, which reduces a person's taxable income figure before the statutory tax rate is applied. There are three tax credits your child should be aware of.

Tuition Credit

The federal tuition credit is calculated as 17 percent of all tuition costs paid in the year. When you factor in the effect of the credit on your provincial income taxes, the total tax savings turn out to be approximately 26 percent of the total tuition paid in the year.

By the way, it doesn't matter if you paid for the tuition instead of your child. The credit must be claimed by your child if she has enough income to use the credit. In most cases, the student's income is so low that she can't claim the full credit for tuition, in which case the credit can be transferred to a parent, grandparent, or spouse. The only catch is that the maximum amount that can be transferred is $5,000.

If a student can't claim a credit for all the tuition paid (because her income is too low), two options are available. The first is to transfer up to $5,000 of tuition to a parent, grandparent, or spouse, who would claim the credit. The second option became available in 1998.

It allows the student to carry forward any unused tuition credits to be claimed in a future year.

Education Credit

In addition to the tuition credit, the student will be able to claim a federal education credit equal to 17 percent of a certain amount. That amount is $200 for each month of full-time enrollment in a qualifying educational program, or $60 per month for a part-time enrollment. The bottom line is that, with the effect on the student's provincial income taxes factored in, the total tax savings is about 26 percent of the base amount (it varies by province). A typical education credit equals 26 percent of $1,600 ($200 times 8 months)—about $416 or so.

As with the tuition credit, if the student can't make use of the full education credit because her income is too low, the credit can be transferred to a parent, grandparent, or spouse, or it can be carried forward for use in a future year.

Student Loan Interest Credit

Here's a credit that could help out a lot of students. It's for interest paid on student loans. This new credit was introduced in the 1998 federal budget, and applies to all interest paid after 1997 on student loans. To qualify, the loan has to have been provided under the *Canada Student Loans Act* or a similar provincial statute. The loan interest has to be paid in the calendar year to claim the credit (accrued interest won't do the trick). The interest credit can be claimed in the year the interest was paid or in any of the five subsequent years. The financial institution lending the money will report the amount of interest paid each year, so you don't have to figure out that messy calculation on your own.

TO MAKE A LONG STORY SHORT:

- Do your child a favour. Make sure she takes maximum advantage of the three credits available to students.

- These three credits are the tuition, education, and student loan interest credits.

Tim's Tip 62: **Make the most of an RRSP—even if you're a student.**

Let me share with you two strategies for students related to the use of an RRSP.

File a Tax Return

Plenty of parents avoid filing tax returns for their kids until the kids' earnings become taxable—that is, until the child's income reaches $7,131 (the basic personal exemption, beginning in 2000). And who can blame a parent for not filing a tax return when it's not required? The problem, however, is that you could be short-changing your child on *future* tax savings if annual tax returns aren't filed.

Here's what I mean. Even though a tax return may not be required until your child reaches a taxable level, you'll do him a favour by fil-ing one anyway if he has "earned income." You see, reporting earned income creates valuable RRSP contribution room, which will lead to tax savings down the road.

When Janice and Peter's son, Lincoln, reached age 13, he made some money by doing chores for other kids around the neighbourhood (until the other kids' parents found out, that is). Nevertheless, he made $350 that year. By reporting that income, he created $63 of RRSP contribution room for himself. No big deal, right? Wrong. Even though that first $63 may not have seemed like much, by the time Lincoln graduated from *university he had accumulated $6,000 of RRSP contribution room. In his first full year of work after graduation, he made that $6,000 contribution, getting a good head start on his retirement savings. And, because of that contribution, he saved himself $2,500 in tax that year.*

Here's an important point to remember: You don't have to claim the deduction for an RRSP contribution in the year you make the contribution. In fact, you can claim the RRSP deduction in any future year. It may make good sense for a student to make a contribution to his own RRSP, provided he has the contribution room and assuming he can spare the cash (perhaps you'd like to help out by giving him money for this purpose), but make sure he saves the deduction for a year when it will provide greater tax savings (that is, when his income is higher).

Making regular RRSP withdrawals for any reason will mean lost contribution room. Here's what I mean: I knew a guy who contributed $10,000 to his RRSP, using up $10,000 of contribution room, then withdrew the funds four months later. Dumb move. The $10,000 of contribution room was effectively lost since it wasn't given back to him when he made the withdrawal. That is, he had no way of putting those funds back into the RRSP without using even more contribution room.

Caution!

Make Withdrawals During No- or Low-Income Years

We found out in Tip 58 in Chapter 6 that tax-free withdrawals under the Life Long Learning plan generally will not hurt your retirement security, since the money you take from your RRSP is put back in over a maximum 10-year period. But what about regular withdrawals from an RRSP to fund an education? (No, I'm not retracting my mantra. I'm still not a big fan of removing RRSP assets for any reason if doing so will jeopardize a secure retirement.)

Regular withdrawals from an RRSP can be used to help fund an education, but because they are fully taxable, the best time to make those withdrawals is during a period when you have no or a low income. The reason is simple: Your tax burden is very light or non-existent in this case. Students, of course, normally fit this bill pretty well—they're broke, no income, no clean underwear (guys only). This scenario assumes, of course, that the student has funds in an RRSP, which could very well be the case if the student is older than the traditional student and is returning to school after being in the workforce.

Let me caution you here. Making RRSP withdrawals that you won't be repaying could have a disastrous impact on the growth of the funds inside your RRSP. You should consider that cost in addition to the tax liability on the withdrawal.

TO MAKE A LONG STORY SHORT:

- It makes a lot of sense to file a tax return for your child if he has earned income because it will create RRSP contribution room for him.

- If you or your child are going to make taxable withdrawals from an RRSP to help pay for an education, try to make them at a time when income is low or non-existent, in addition to the lost contribution room.

Tim's Tip 63: **Put a child to work in order to claim a number of tax benefits.**

I'm not talking here about hiring your three-year-old to do hard labour. But I do want you to be aware of three strategies that will allow you to split income with a child and put money in her hands for an education to boot.

Pay an Allowance to a Working Child

Let's face it, you're looking forward to the day when your child will be out there earning her own spending money. What if I were to tell you that paying your child an allowance makes sense once she is earning money? Here's why: Giving your child an allowance when she's working will free up her earnings for investment. And when your child invests her own income, the attribution rules don't apply. This strategy, then, will allow investment income to be taxed in your child's hands when it might otherwise have been taxed in your hands at a higher rate.

Pay Your Child to Help with a Family Move

If your family is moving and you're entitled to claim moving expenses, why not pay your adult child to help in the move? Hey, somebody's got to drive the truck and move that furniture. It might as well be a family member. You'll not only keep the money in the family, but you'll be entitled to a tax deduction for the payment made—subject, of course, to the usual moving expense rules (which I talk about in my book *Winning the Tax Game*). Your child will have to report the income, but she's not likely to pay much tax, if any, when her income is low. A side benefit is that she will be entitled to RRSP contribution room on the earnings.

There's nothing quite like moving income directly from your tax return to your child's, and that's what you'd be accomplishing with this strategy.

Pay Your Child for Babysitting

Try this idea on for size if you have children aged 16 or under, and another child who is age 18 or over. Consider paying your adult child (the one who is 18 or over in the tax year) to babysit the younger kids who are age 16 or under. Babysitting fees, like other child care expenses, may be deductible if they were paid to allow you to earn income. Here's how it works. You're entitled to a deduction for any babysitting fees paid to your adult child, and that child will report the amounts as income. If her income is low, however, there's a pretty good chance she will pay little or no tax on that income.

This strategy moves income directly from your tax return to your child's, and it provides your child with earned income that will create RRSP contribution room.

TO MAKE A LONG STORY SHORT:

- Splitting income with your child will save your family taxes.

- Consider the following strategies: pay your working child an allowance to free up her income for investment; pay your adult child to help the family move; pay your adult child to babysit the younger kids.

Investing for the Future

A sure way to make a million bucks is to start with $10 million, then invest in a hot tip. If you haven't got $10 million to start with, then my advice here should get you—and your child—to that $1 million mark, even if it does take a number of years. Even though your child is still young, there's no better time to learn the importance and principles of proper investing. Why? Because your child already has the most important resource that any investor could ask for: *time.* Your child may not be able to invest much today, but any start is better than no start.

By the way, how are your own investments doing? You'll stand to benefit from these principles too. And remember, there is no better way to teach your kids about this stuff than to lead by example.

Tim's Tip 64: **Invest 10 percent of your take-home pay monthly.**

There is just one problem with working for a living: You've only got so many hours in a year that you can work. If you hope to build wealth, you're going to have to take advantage of two resources over the long run: your time and your money. In fact, there's no better way to build wealth over the long term than to set up a regular investment program. Eventually, your investments could provide a greater annual income than your employment.

So make investing a regular habit. Set aside 10 percent of your take-home pay each month. It's a simple process to set in motion. First, open an investment account with a reputable financial adviser, or at your local bank. (If you're going to open an account at your bank, you had better feel comfortable with your own ability to choose investments since bank staff are not known for their investment knowledge). Second, arrange for 10 percent of your monthly take-home pay to be transferred from your bank account to your investment account on a monthly basis. Treat these payments as though they were mortgage payments. That is, these payments should be mandatory and not open to negotiation.

This is known as "paying yourself first." Most people go about investing in the wrong manner. They pay for all the

Action Step

The concept of investing 10 percent of income on a monthly basis is not new. It's a strategy espoused by many experts—including David Chilton in his book *The Wealthy Barber*. I usually recommend investing 10 percent of take-home pay, but if you or your child have the ability to invest 10 percent of gross income, you'll be even further ahead. In fact, investing 10 percent of gross income rather than take-home pay will result in over 50 percent more in savings after 20 years, assuming a 9 percent rate of return.

things they've got to pay for each month, and if there's anything left over, it's invested. The problem? There's never anything left over to invest! Paying yourself first is the solution. You'll be amazed at how painless it can be. If you're like most Canadians, you won't even miss the money transferred to your investment account monthly.

L*indsay is 15 years old. Last year, she earned $2,000 working part-time at the movie theatre. She wasn't taxed on the income since it was low enough not to be taxable. She set aside $200 (10 percent) last year in equity mutual funds. This year, she expects to do the same. If she were to simply set aside $200 annually for the next 50 years until retirement at age 65, she would have $123,934 at the end of that time, assuming an 8 percent return on her money annually. If she didn't touch this money and simply let it grow for another 20 years until her death at, say, age 85, the investment account would be worth $577,651. Not bad for an investment of a mere $200 annually to age 65. The fact is, she plans to invest much more than just $200 annually once she graduates from university. The point is, even a little can go a long way over the long term.*

What are these investments to be used for? Nothing—at the moment. The idea is to build a large enough investment portfolio that you can eventually make use of the annual income generated on the portfolio. But this income shouldn't be accessed yet. Let the account grow. Choose good quality long-term equity mutual funds as the core of the portfolio and forget about the account. Don't check the values daily. Check them quarterly.

TO MAKE A LONG STORY SHORT:

- The route to wealth is to take advantage of your two key resources: your time and your money. Eventually, your money invested could provide a greater annual income than your employment.

- Invest 10 percent of your take-home pay monthly by setting up a "pay yourself first" plan with a financial adviser, or your bank.

- Don't touch your 10 percent account except to invest more money. It's there for the long term.

Tim's Tip 65: Avoid timing the market by sticking with good quality long-term investments.

The most successful investors in the world will tell you that the only sure way to build wealth is to buy good equity investments and stick with them for the long term. Trying to time the stock market is crazy. Sure, many of us have friends who have made money over the course of a day or a week by investing in a hot tip or a high-flying hi-tech stock, but over the long term, those folks will be lucky to beat the returns you can experience by simply buying quality equity investments and holding them. It may not be as exciting as "day-trading," but it sure is a lot more reliable.

Peter Lynch is one of the world's most successful investors. He is vice-chairman of Fidelity Management & Research Company—the investment advisory arm of Fidelity Investments. Fidelity is a household name when it comes to mutual funds. Here's what Lynch has to say about market timing:

If you had invested $1,000 in the S&P 500 in 1978 and stayed invested through 1997, your investment would be worth $21,750. However, if you missed the best 15 months (less than 7 percent of the months) your investment would only be worth $6,010. The same holds true for Canada—$1,000 invested in the

TSE 300 in 1978 would be worth $12,527; however, missing the best 15 months drops it down to $4,334. Trying to predict which day or month or even years the market will be up is impossible. Even the people who get lucky and make one good prediction can't repeat it. You could flip a coin and do as well. However, what we do know is that over the long term, the market has historically gone up. In order to experience the potential benefits of the market, you need to be in the market.

The moral of the story? It's time in the market, not timing the market that will produce the best investment results over the long term.

TO MAKE A LONG STORY SHORT:

- Trying to guess the direction of the stock market, or a particular stock, in order to profit from the market is a fool's game.

- The only sure way to build wealth is to choose quality equity investments as the core of your portfolio, and hold them for the long term.

- Peter Lynch, one of the world's greatest investment analysts, is one of many experts who adopt a buy and hold strategy.

Tim's Tip 66: **Understand the investments you're making, or don't make them at all.**

The great investor Peter Lynch, whom I introduced in Tip 65, believes that everyone ought to be able to tell a friend in a 30-second elevator ride why he owns a certain stock, bond, or mutual fund. The reason? Because this demonstrates that you understand what you're doing. This philosophy will pretty much shoot down any strategy that involves investing in a hot tip, because it requires that you do your homework before putting your hard-earned cash into any investment.

Think about all the work that you go to when buying a new car. You'll read consumer reports, surf the Internet for information, ask friends for their thoughts, and check with someone who really knows cars for their opinion. You'll probably stick to a brand name with a good reputation. Why would you do anything less with your investments?

If it's mutual funds you're looking to invest in, there's no shortage of good books on the market. Some of my good friends write books on the subject: Duff Young writes *FundMonitor*, Riley Moynes and Michael Nairne write *Top Funds*, and Gordon Pape writes his annual *Mutual Funds Guide*. There are others available also—just check the shelves at your local book store. These guides will provide you with all you need to know about which mutual funds to choose—and why. Of course, a financial adviser can also provide you with advice in this area.

Investing in individual stocks, bonds, or other securities can be a more difficult task, although equally or more rewarding over the long term than mutual funds if you invest only in securities that you understand and have carefully researched, or have an adviser with access to good research. Here's a caveat, however: Before investing in individual securities, you've got to know what makes an investment attractive, and when to sell it. Alternatively, you should have an adviser with these capabilities. If you're not comfortable with this task, stick to mutual funds.

TO MAKE A LONG STORY SHORT:

- You ought to be able to tell a friend in a 30-second elevator ride why you own a certain stock, bond, or mutual fund. This demonstrates that you know what you're doing.

- Understanding your investments will take some research. You'll find a number of good books on mutual funds to help with your decision making. Individual securities selection (primarily stocks and bonds) will take more knowledge and effort to research unless you have an adviser with these capabilities.

Tim's Tip 67: **Diversify your investments through asset allocation to minimize risks.**

Don't put all your eggs in one basket. You've heard it before and it makes complete sense when applied to your investments. How should you diversify your investments? Through a tool called "asset allocation." I first talked about asset allocation in Tip 27 where we looked at appropriate asset allocations when saving for a child's education. Asset allocation is really the process of deciding where to put all those eggs, since you don't want to hold them in just one basket.

A study by Brinson, Singer, and Beebower, which appeared in the *Financial Analysts Journal* in 1991, revealed that 91.5 percent of the returns of a given investment portfolio are determined by the allocation of your assets among the three broad investment categories: equities (primarily stocks), fixed-income (primarily bonds), and cash. In other words, your decision about how much to hold in each of these categories will do more to impact your investment results than even the selection of individual stocks, bonds, and mutual funds.

The percentage of your portfolio that is held in stocks versus bonds or cash will depend on a number of factors, including your objectives, tolerance for risk, time frame for investing (i.e., a person investing to buy a home in two years will choose more conservative investments than someone investing for retirement 30 years away), age, liquidity requirements, tax efficiency, among other factors.

The general rule of thumb is that equity investments (primarily stocks and mutual funds that invest in stocks) will outperform cash and bonds over the long term. While this is generally true, there are exceptions to the rule. There have been 10-year periods where bonds have outperformed stocks, and even a few 10-year periods where cash has done the same. Consider this:

- For the month following the stock market correction on October 19, 1987, the S&P 500 and TSE 300 were down 21.5 percent and 22.5 percent respectively. Intermediate government bonds were up

3 percent in the United States that month, and mid-term bonds were up 6.5 percent that month.

- From 1973 to 1982 the S&P 500 compound annual return was 6.7 percent while Treasury bills returned 8.5 percent in the United States.

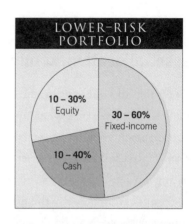

An asset allocation that includes fixed-income investments and cash will take advantage of the returns offered by those categories when they do happen to outperform equities. What should your asset allocation look like? You'll have to decide that on your own or in conjunction with a financial adviser. But take a look at the pie charts on this page. Each chart illustrates a portfolio appropriate to a particular level of risk tolerance.

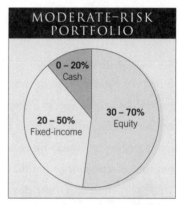

Let me make two final comments on this issue of diversification. First, some of your investments should be in foreign content. I've talked about this before in Tip 27. Canada represents just under 3 percent of total world markets (the United States represents 45 percent!). In addition,

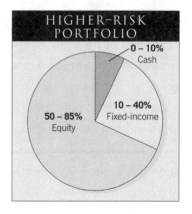

Canadian securities are subject to certain risks that you won't find in other economies. In particular, our economy is resource-based, which means that our markets fluctuate heavily with changes in resource

prices, and there is also political uncertainty with the never-ending Québec separation issue, which does not bode well for the foreign demand for Canadian securities. Protect yourself from these risks by diversifying internationally, holding at least 40 percent of your portfolio in foreign content. (There is, of course, a restriction of 20 percent foreign content inside your RRSP, although there are ways to effectively hold more foreign content than this. My book *Winning the Tax Game* provides some ideas in this regard.)

Second, provided your investment objectives haven't changed, stick to your well-reasoned asset allocation and avoid the temptation to jump to a new allocation simply because it appears that one segment of the market is outperforming the others. You might just find, for example, that the minute you jump into small-cap equities (stocks in smaller companies) because they had been doing well, the scales could tip the other way and the large-cap stocks you moved out of might be in favour. This brings me back to the principle that market timing is a very tough game to win. Your asset allocation should change only when your investment objectives have changed.

TO MAKE A LONG STORY SHORT:

- Don't put all your investment eggs in one basket. Allocate them among the three categories of investments: equities, fixed-income, and cash.

- Asset allocation among these categories will have a greater impact on your investment returns than even the selection of individual securities.

- Diversify internationally.

- Don't change your asset allocation unless your investment objectives have changed.

WINNING THE EDUCATION SAVINGS GAME

Paying for the education of that special child in your life is going to be easier if both you and your child exercise proper financial planning strategies. In this chapter, I've introduced to you some key strategies in the areas of cash management, debt management, tax planning, and investment planning. Refer now to the Education Planning Tip Sheet at the front of the book and make note of those tips you'd like to follow up further.

With the conclusion of this chapter, you now have all the tools you're going to need to put a proper education plan in place. You now understand the five methods to pay for your child's education that we talked about in Chapters 3 and 4: begging, borrowing, stealing, sweating, and saving. In Chapter 5 you came to understand the rules around RESPs and CESGs, and tips and traps to watch for, and you learned about alternative strategies like in-trust accounts, family trusts, and life insurance policies in Chapter 6.

You might still have some unanswered questions about RESPs, CESGs, and in-trust accounts in particular. These are the most common vehicles in saving for a child's education. I've devoted the final chapter, Chapter 8, to answering many questions that have come my way over the last couple of years, and you stand a good chance at finding your answers there.

In closing, I applaud you for being concerned enough about the education of the child in your life to read this book. My hope for your child is that he or she will benefit significantly from the things you have learned here. And if that happens to be the case, I'd be pleased to hear from you. I can be reached at tim@waterstreet.ca. Take care.

RAISING A HAND IN CLASS:

FREQUENTLY ASKED QUESTIONS

Learning is all about questions, not answers.

8

I think it's safe to say that over the last couple of years I've heard and seen it all with respect to registered education savings plans (RESPs), Canadian Education Savings Grants (CESGs), and other methods of saving for a child's education. And as part of an extended family with 13 kids (18, if you count the brothers-in-law), I've heard most questions that can be asked about these issues. Not to mention the questions on saving for a child's education that I've received in the form of letters and e-mail messages from readers of my "Tax Matters" column in the *Globe and*

Mail and from the hundreds of financial advisers across the country to whom I've spoken over the last couple of years.

As a result, I have managed to compile 99 questions and answers on RESPs, CESGs, and other related issues. If you have question 100, and the answer isn't here, I'd be surprised. But if you can't find the answer here, try visiting my firm's Web site at www.waterstreet.ca. Our Web site has a discussion forum called "Tax Talk" that you'll find helpful. Simply ask your question there, and you're bound to get a quick answer. You can also leave a question in the "Mailbag" area of the Web site, and the professionals at my firm—The WaterStreet Group—will consider posting an answer on the site.

Okay, let's hop to it—your questions and answers. I've divided the questions into eight categories:

- general information
- subscribers
- contributions
- beneficiaries
- withdrawals
- Canada Education Savings Grants
- investments
- in-trust accounts and other vehicles.

General Information

1. *What types of RESPs are there?* RESPs come in two general types: self-directed plans and group plans. Self-directed plans usually offer more flexibility in terms of investment options and the timing of payments from the plan. Group plans, often called scholarship trusts or pooled trust plans, don't normally offer the same flexibility. (See Tip 36 in Chapter 5.) Both self-directed and group plans can also be split into two types of plans: individual and family plans. (See Tip 37 in Chapter 5.)

2. *Where can I open an RESP?* You can open an RESP at any number of places that offer financial services. Most commonly, you'll find RESPs at one of the following:

- mutual fund companies
- brokerage firms
- financial planning firms
- banks
- trust companies
- credit unions
- scholarship trust organizations
- life insurance companies

Generally, each of the institutions above will offer a self-directed plan with a varying array of investment options (except for scholarship trust organizations, which don't provide investment options). See Appendix B for a list of firms offering RESPs.

3. *Can an RESP remain open forever?* Nope. An RESP has a maximum lifespan of 25 years. It has to be closed down on or before December 31 of the year that includes the 25th anniversary of the plan. So if a plan is set up in 2000, it must be terminated on or before December 31, 2025. By the way, contributions to an RESP can only continue until December 31 of the year that includes the 21st anniversary of the plan (December 31, 2021, in my example), even though the plan itself can continue for 4 years beyond that point.

4. *Can assets be transferred from one RESP to another without any problems?* You won't normally face a tax hit for transferring assets from one RESP to another. But there are five potential exceptions to a hassle-free, tax-free rollover:

- *If you exceed the lifetime $42,000 limit.* If the transfer of assets from one RESP to another involves a change in beneficiaries, some of the new beneficiaries under the new (transferee) plan may have enough new assets allocated to them that they will exceed the

$42,000 lifetime contribution limit allowable for each beneficiary. This isn't a problem if at least one of the beneficiaries of the first RESP is also a beneficiary of the new RESP. Nor will it be a problem if at least one of the beneficiaries of the new RESP is under age 21 and a sibling of a beneficiary of the old RESP.

- *If you transfer assets from an individual plan to certain family plans.* You cannot transfer assets from an RESP that is an individual plan (a single-beneficiary plan) to a family plan (where all beneficiaries are related to the subscriber by blood or adoption), if the beneficiaries of the family plan have all attained age 21. This restriction relates to the government's policy that contributions for a beneficiary of a family plan must stop once the beneficiary has reached age 21.

- *If you transfer from a plan that has made accumulated income payments.* An RESP is not entitled to receive a direct transfer of assets from another RESP where the transferor RESP has already made an accumulated income payment (AIP). An AIP is a payment of the accumulated income in the plan (not the original contributions) made to the subscriber of the plan.

- *If you are required to repay CESGs.* The rules say that you must repay CESGs if your transfer from one RESP to another involves a change of beneficiaries or a partial transfer of funds from one plan to the other. To avoid having to repay the CESGs when transferring from one plan to another, you'd better make sure that you don't change the beneficiaries and that all the assets of the first RESP move to the new plan.

- *If your scholarship trust plan imposes fees.* Some scholarship trust plans may not allow a transfer from their plan to another company's RESP without administrative penalties or fees. Check it out first.

Okay, I can hear the groaning from here. I know these rules are a handful, and nearly impossible to remember. Let me sum it all up for you in a simple sentence: You'll avoid any problems transferring from one RESP to the next if you don't change the beneficiaries of the plan and if you move 100 percent of the assets to the new RESP. That's it in a nutshell. If the transfer you're contemplating is more complicated than this, read through the rules carefully—and get some professional tax advice if you're talking about a lot of money.

5. *Who is related by blood or adoption for the purpose of family plans?* You'll recall that a family plan is an RESP that is permitted to have more than one beneficiary, provided each beneficiary is connected to the subscriber of the plan by blood or adoption. What does "connected by blood or adoption" mean?

The law says that two people are connected by a blood relationship if one is the brother, sister, child, grandchild, great-grandchild, or other descendent of the other. (That is, you're related by blood to your siblings, parents, grandparents, child, grandchild, and so on—both up and down the line.) Relationship by adoption works the same way. If you've been adopted, your adoptive siblings, parents, grandparents, children, and grandchildren are considered related to you by adoption. Notice that under the law you're not considered related by blood or adoption to your aunts or uncles or your nieces and nephews. And further, you're not related by blood or adoption to yourself or your spouse.

6. *What kind of schools and programs qualify to entitle a beneficiary to receive education assistance payments (EAPs) from an RESP?* For your child to receive EAPs from an RESP, she has to be enrolled in a postsecondary educational institution and a qualifying educational program. By "postsecondary educational institution," Revenue Canada means just about any university, college, or similar institution. The tax law doesn't actually list specific schools that qualify, but simply refers to lists contained in other legislation, such as the *Canada Student Loans Act*, the *Canada Student Financial Assistance Act*, and similar legislation in Québec. The tax law also considers universities and colleges outside Canada to qualify if the student enrolls in a postsecondary-level course of not less than 13 consecutive weeks' duration.

As I said, it's also important to be enrolled in a "qualifying educational program." A qualifying program is generally defined as one that is not less than 3 consecutive weeks in duration and requires the student to spend not less than 10 hours per week on courses or work in the program. By the way, if your child enrolls in a program of less than 3 months, the amount that can be withdrawn from the RESP will be limited to the cost of tuition plus $300 per week of study (or a higher amount if approved by Human Resources Development Canada on a case-by-case basis).

7. *What happens if an RESP matures after 25 years but it still contains money?* Your child has to use withdrawals from an RESP (that is, the EAPs) to pay his qualifying postsecondary education costs. If he has already finished his education and the RESP is about to mature with assets still in the plan, it could spell bad news. In this case, you can still withdraw the assets yourself as the subscriber, and while any capital in the plan can come out tax-free, any accumulated income payments will be taxed in your hands and a 20 percent penalty will apply. Ideally, you'd want to set up the withdrawals so that all the accumulated income is used by the last year of the child's postsecondary schooling.

In fact, it may be best if the child withdraws most of his EAPs before the calendar year in which he graduates and starts working full-time. Why? Because tax on withdrawn income could be higher in the last year of education if the student is also reporting higher employment income in that year than ever before.

As for the Canada Education Savings Grants (CESGs), you can count on repaying whatever grant money is still in the RESP if the assets are still in the plan when it winds up after 25 years. CESG funds must be repaid any time money is withdrawn for non-education purposes.

8. *If I have more than one child, is it better to set up an individual plan for each child or a family plan with multiple beneficiaries?* It's commonly felt that a family plan makes lots of sense, since you can name all your children as beneficiaries, and if one of them doesn't go to school, you can allow the others to use all the assets in the plan for their schooling. So you don't really lose anything if at least one child pursues a postsecondary education. I'm convinced, however, that an individual plan makes the most sense, since it provides the most flexibility in terms of changing beneficiaries later (see Tip 37 in Chapter 5).

Subscribers

9. *Who can be an RESP subscriber?* Our tax law makes it clear that a subscriber must be an individual. A trust or corporation cannot be a subscriber to an RESP. A subscriber can be any individual who chooses to set up an RESP for a beneficiary. There's no need for the subscriber to be related to the beneficiary in the case of an individual plan. For the most part, however, the subscriber is usually a parent, grandparent, other relative, or friend of the RESP beneficiary. Most often, there is just one subscriber to an RESP, although it's possible to have joint subscribers when they are spouses.

10. *Who should be the RESP subscriber?* This question is important. From a practical point of view, it's most common for the parents of a child to be the subscribers to an RESP. It may be the case, however, that someone else is also interested in contributing to an RESP for your child. In this case, the subscribers should communicate with each other to make sure the total contributions for the child do not exceed $4,000 annually and $42,000 in the child's lifetime. (See Tip 40 in Chapter 5.)

11. *Can more than one person be named as the subscriber on an RESP?* Yes, joint subscribers are allowed, but only where the joint subscribers are spouses.

12. *Can the subscriber be changed once the plan has been set up?* Generally the subscriber can't be changed after the plan has been set up. But, as with most tax rules, there are certain exceptions. Changes are allowed in the following situations:

- *Marriage breakdown:* If a spouse or former spouse acquires the subscriber's rights under an RESP due to marriage breakdown, that person can become the RESP subscriber. For this change to take place, the rights must be acquired by the new subscriber under a written separation or divorce agreement, or pursuant to a decree, order, or judgment of a competent tribunal.

- *Death of subscriber:* In the event of the death of a subscriber, the deceased's estate may become the subscriber. As an alternative, our tax law allows the surviving spouse or any other heir who makes a contribution to the plan after the subscriber's death to replace the original subscriber. (See also question 18.)

By the way, check the terms and conditions of your RESP as well, in case there are restrictions under the terms of your particular plan that might prevent a change in subscriber.

13. *Can the subscriber to an RESP be a minor?* Interestingly enough, the *Income Tax Act* does not place any limits on the age of RESP subscribers. But you can bet that the issuer of the RRSP will have policies related to age, and it's unlikely that any RESP promoter would be willing to enter into a contract with a minor. The bottom line? Don't count on your child being able to subscribe to an RESP until she reaches the age of majority.

14. *Can an adult subscribe to an RESP for himself to take advantage of the tax-free growth inside the plan?* In the case of a family plan, our tax law requires that beneficiaries be under age 21 on the date they become beneficiaries. As a result, a person over age

21 cannot become a beneficiary of a family plan. The beneficiary of an individual plan, however, can be any age. So it is possible for an adult to subscribe to an RESP for himself. An adult beneficiary, however, should not expect to receive any Canada Education Savings Grants from the government, because it's not going to happen.

Keep in mind that to receive educational assistance payments from the plan, it's necessary to enroll in a qualifying educational program at a postsecondary educational institution. If that program is less than three months in duration, the amount that can be withdrawn from the plan will be limited to the cost of tuition plus $300 per week of the program.

15. Can a Canadian resident subscribe to an RESP for a non-resident child? The *Income Tax Act* does not require that the beneficiary of an RESP be resident in Canada, so yes, it's possible for a non-resident child to be the beneficiary of an RESP. In addition, the *Income Tax Act* allows the beneficiary to attend a postsecondary institution outside of Canada, so the child's attendance at a foreign school should not pose a problem. CESGs, however, are only available to Canadian-resident kids. In addition, the taxable portion of any payments from an RESP to a non-resident child will attract a withholding tax of 25 percent.

You'll also need to consider the tax implications in the child's country of residence. Payments from the RESP could be fully taxed (income and capital portions), partially taxed (income portion only), or tax-free in the other country. If the payments are taxed in the country of the child's residence, it's likely that a foreign tax credit is available in that country for the 25 percent withholding tax paid to Revenue Canada. Whether an RESP is the right vehicle for a non-resident child depends on the tax implications in the child's country of residence.

16. Can a non-resident subscribe to an RESP for a Canadian-resident child? While the *Income Tax Act* does not require that the subscriber of an RESP be resident in Canada, two other issues may prevent this strategy from being useful. Here's what I mean. First, while the income inside an RESP will grow tax-free in Canada, the country where the subscriber is resident is likely to want its share of the income earned in the RESP on an annual basis. After all, an RESP is a tax-deferred plan in Canada, but it won't hold its tax-deferred status in the country of the subscriber's residence.

Second, if the non-resident has a self-directed RESP, the Canadian financial adviser or RESP promoter may be unable to advise the non-resident on investment issues, and may be unable to purchase or sell investments in the RESP on behalf of the non-resident—due to securities law. The non-resident may be better off giving funds to a Canadian resident who can in turn subscribe to an RESP for the child, or setting up an education savings plan in her own country of residence for the child.

17. Can a non-resident subscribe to an RESP for a non-resident child, and if so, is there any advantage to this strategy? The answer to this question is really a combination of my answers to questions 15 and 16. There's nothing in our tax law to prevent a non-resident from subscribing to an RESP, and there's nothing to prevent a non-resident from being a beneficiary. The drawbacks, however, are as follows:

- CESGs are not paid into the RESPs of non-resident beneficiaries.
- A withholding tax of 25 percent will apply to taxable payments made out of the plan to the child.
- Payments from the plan are likely to face tax in the country of the beneficiary's residence (which, combined with the withholding tax, will complicate the tax filings for the beneficiary).
- The country of the subscriber's residence is likely to tax the income earned inside the RESP annually.
- Canadian RESP promoters and financial advisers may not be permitted to provide investment advice to or carry out instructions from a non-resident because of the securities laws.

The bottom line? A non-resident subscriber could set up an RESP for a non-resident beneficiary, but why in the world would you want to? The drawbacks are too numerous.

18. ***What happens if the subscriber to the RESP dies?*** A subscriber to an RESP has acquired certain rights. They include, most significantly, the right to take back any capital contributed to the RESP. These rights form part of the property of the subscriber, and will form part of the subscriber's estate if he should die.

The treatment of any contributions to the RESP depends on the deceased's will. If the deceased subscriber did not specifically address the issue of the contributions to the RESP in the will, then the deceased's executor presumably has the authority to manage the RESP, including withdrawing any capital amounts, until the estate is wound up and the property of the deceased is passed to the heirs in accordance with the will.

Since the rights to the capital of the RESP represent property of the deceased, one or more of the heirs will have received these subscriber rights once all the deceased's property has been distributed in accordance with the will. Any of these heirs could step into the shoes of the deceased as subscriber. In fact, our tax law says that, after the death of a subscriber, any other heir (including the estate of the deceased subscriber) who makes contributions to the RESP for the beneficiary will become the new subscriber. As the new subscriber, this heir would be entitled to withdraw the capital of the RESP, would be taxed on any accumulated income payments that come out of the plan should the beneficiary of the RESP not attend postsecondary school, and would assume any other benefits, rights, or obligations that accrue to a subscriber.

If a subscriber has specific wishes for the capital contributed to the RESP (that the beneficiary of the RESP should receive the capital, for example), it would be best to spell them out in the will so that the executor and heirs understand them. (See Tip 45 in Chapter 5 for more.)

Contributions

19. *What is the maximum amount I can contribute to an RESP?*
Subscribers can contribute up to $4,000 each year to an RESP, for each beneficiary. So, if you have three kids and contribute the maximum each year for each of them, you will be making $12,000 in contributions annually. The lifetime maximum for each beneficiary is $42,000 in contributions. So if you were to make the maximum contribution to an RESP each year, you would have contributed $40,000 after 10 years, bringing you close to the maximum $42,000. In the 11th year, you could make a final $2,000 contribution to bring the total to $42,000.

20. *Are contributions to an RESP tax-deductible as they are with an RRSP?* No, you can't deduct RESP contributions. Don't let this fool you into thinking that these plans are therefore a bad deal. On the contrary, you'll still enjoy tax-free growth over the years on the capital contributed to the RESP. In addition, when the accumulated income in the plan is withdrawn by your child when he attends postsecondary school, your child—not you—will pay the tax on that income. This is income splitting, and it's an effective method of reducing a family's overall tax burden.

21. *Is there a deadline for contributions to an RESP?* Your RESP contribution for a particular tax year must be made during that calendar year. Unlike with an RRSP, you're not entitled to make a contribution to an RESP for a particular year within the 60 days following that year's end. In fact, you'll do your child a favour by making contributions early in the year. By doing so, you'll provide maximum growth inside the plan, you'll provide a larger education nest-egg for your child's education, and you'll also maximize the income splitting potential provided by RESPs.

22. *Is a minimum contribution required to open an RESP?*
The *Income Tax Act* sets out no minimum contribution limits.

Individual RESP promoters, however, may have minimum restrictions under the rules of their plans. Be sure to ask before subscribing.

23. Can a subscriber contribute to the plan after the beneficiary begins receiving educational assistance payments from the plan? Sure, but you have to remember that contributions must cease by the end of the year in which the 21st anniversary of the plan falls, and the plan must be terminated by the end of the year in which the 25th anniversary of the plan falls. In addition, contributions to a family plan for a beneficiary must stop once the beneficiary reaches age 21.

24. Can I carry forward the $4,000 RESP contribution entitlement if I don't make a contribution in a given year? I wish I had better news for you here. The answer is no. An RESP does not work like your RRSP, which allows unlimited carrying forward of unused contribution room. The $4,000 contribution limit remains the same each year, whether or not you made contributions in previous years. Don't confuse this $4,000 limit with the $2,000 Canada Education Savings Grant (CESG) room that your child receives each year. That $2,000 CESG room can be carried forward for future use if it's not used in a given year. I'll talk more about CESG room later.

25. Are there penalties for over-contributing to an RESP? You bet there are. The subscriber can expect to pay a penalty tax of 1 percent of the excess contributions for each month the over-contribution is still in the RESP at the end of the month. Revenue Canada may waive the penalty in certain situations, which include reasonable error, or if the penalty is excessive. And the penalty could be excessive in some cases, especially if you exchange one beneficiary for another.

You see, when a new beneficiary is named, every contribution made for the former beneficiary is now considered to be a contribution for the new beneficiary, effective from the date those contributions were originally made for the former beneficiary. If the new beneficiary has already had maximum contributions made on her behalf, these new contributions could result in an over-contribution problem (unless the new beneficiary is under age 21 and both the former and new beneficiaries are related by blood or adoption to the subscriber). The penalty on these new contributions will be calculated going back to the date the contributions were made for the former beneficiary. Follow me?

Suffice it to say there's a chance the tax collector will go easy on you if the penalties seem excessive. Just ask for relief pursuant to subsection 204.91(2) of the *Income Tax Act*. (See Tip 46 in Chapter 5.)

26. Should I borrow to make RESP contributions? Sure. There's nothing to stop you from borrowing to make an RESP contribution. But don't count on deducting the interest costs for tax purposes. Borrowing can make sense when it's getting close to the end of the calendar year and you want to make a contribution so that you don't lose the opportunity to contribute for the year. (Remember, the $4,000 annual contribution limit is not carried forward if you fail to contribute in a year). In addition, by borrowing to contribute at that time, you'll ensure CESG room is not carried forward. If too much CESG room goes unused and is carried forward for too long, you may never be able to use up the room, and you'll lose the opportunity for some CESG payments at that point.

But I don't recommend that you take out a long-term loan for RESP purposes. Borrowing makes the most sense when you can pay off the loan within one year.

27. Is the interest on the loan tax-deductible when I borrow to contribute to an RESP? Nice try, but you're out of luck. The fact is, paragraph 18(11)(h) of the *Income Tax Act* specifically says that no deduction is allowed for interest when the borrowed money is contributed to an RESP. Sorry about that. But I still think borrowing for RESP contributions can make sense in some situations (see question 26).

28. *What happens if I stop contributing to an RESP?* If you don't contribute to an RESP in one year, you can't carry the $4,000 annual contribution limit forward and make a catch-up contribution in a subsequent year. The good news, however, is that you'll still be able to reach the maximum $42,000 lifetime contribution limit, even if you don't contribute every year. After all, it only takes 11 years of maximum contributions to hit the $42,000 mark.

You should be aware, however, that certain group plans (scholarship trust RESPs) could give you a hassle if you fail to make contributions in accordance with the plan's terms and conditions. In a worst-case scenario, you might just forfeit the income inside the RESP if your contributions are not made on time. Be sure to check the terms of your plan if you've subscribed to a group plan.

29. *Can contributions be made by trusts and corporations?* The subscriber to an RESP must be an individual. Trusts and corporations are not permitted to be subscribers to an RESP, with one exception. If a subscriber dies, her estate (which is a trust) can continue to contribute to the plan. If you've already established and funded a formal trust for your child, you'll have to find other sources of funding for an RESP.

If you're a small business owner operating through a corporation, you won't be able to make payments directly from the company to an RESP. You could, however, borrow from your corporation to make a contribution as the individual subscriber. The loan from the company will not be included in your income provided you repay it by the end of your company's fiscal year following the fiscal year you take out the loan.

30. *Can a subscriber contribute to an RESP for the entire life of the plan?* Contributions by a subscriber can only be made for the first 21 years the plan is in existence. Specifically, contributions can be

made up until December 31 of the year in which the 21st anniversary of the plan falls. The plan itself can exist for 25 years, but contributions will have to cease 4 years before that time.

There's another restriction here. In the case of a family plan, contributions can only be made up until the 21st birthday of the beneficiary. (This restriction doesn't apply to individual plans, although the general rule still applies that contributions cannot extend beyond the 21st year of the plan itself.)

31. Can a person contribute to an RESP if he is not the subscriber to the plan? Nope. Only a subscriber can contribute to a plan. Suppose, for example, that you set up an RESP for your child, and then your parents (your child's grandparents) also want to contribute. Your parents would not be able to contribute to the RESP you have set up. They would have to set up and become subscribers to an RESP of their own. They could still name your child as beneficiary on that second RESP, but each contributor must be a subscriber. Joint subscribers are allowed, but only when they are spouses.

32. Can I designate the contributions to my family plan as contributions for my oldest child in the plan first? I understand the concern here. If your oldest child will be attending school before the others, it would be nice to earmark the contributions to the plan for that child first when you've named more than one child as beneficiary in the plan. The good news is that with a family plan there's no need to worry about this type of allocation. You're entitled to make contributions to a family plan as long as you don't exceed the aggregate contribution limits of all the beneficiaries combined. So if you have three children as beneficiaries in the plan, you can contribute $12,000 annually ($4,000 X 3 beneficiaries) and $126,000 over the lifetime of the plan ($42,000 X 3 beneficiaries).

When it comes to taking educational assistance payments (payments of the accumulated income, but not the contributions) out of the plan for the beneficiaries, you have complete discretion to decide which kids will get how much. There's no need to split the accumulated income in the plan evenly.

As for the contributions you made to the RESP, they cannot be split in just any fashion if the funds are to be used for educational purposes. The contributions must stick with the child for whom you made the contributions. Of course, you do have the right to take them back at any time. Once the capital is back in your hands, you can do with it as you please, including using it for the education of your oldest child first. Taking the capital back, however, will likely require you to repay the Canada Education Savings Grant money related to the funds withdrawn (see question 65).

33. *What should be my first priority—my mortgage, my RRSP, or my child's RESP?* There's no doubt that these three savings priorities present a conflict for those with children and a mortgage. There may not be one right answer for everyone, but I can provide some general guidelines to help you make an educated decision.

First, your retirement must be your number one priority. Consider carefully whether you're on track in saving enough income for your retirement. If you're not sure how well you're doing in this area, visit a financial adviser who will do the calculations for you. Once you've looked after your retirement, then you can worry about your child's education and your mortgage.

Opinions will differ as to which priority should be your next. My feeling is that your child's education comes next. Your mortgage is going to look after itself over the course of time, and chances are pretty good that the mortgage will be paid off by the time you're ready to retire (which is what really matters, in my view). Sure, you can save some interest costs by paying off the mortgage more quickly, but your child's education is not far away and the costs of education are rising. You need to start saving quickly to help in any meaningful way.

If you're intent on paying off your mortgage before saving for education, at least take advantage of the CESG payments available from the government by contributing $2,000 annually to an RESP.

Finally, do your best to have your cake and eat it too. Take the tax savings from your RRSP deduction each year and use them to make a contribution to an RESP and to pay down your mortgage.

Beneficiaries

34. Who can be a beneficiary of an RESP? It depends on whether you're talking about an individual plan or a family plan. The beneficiary of an individual-plan RESP can be absolutely anyone. You can even name yourself as beneficiary. Family plans work a little differently. Family plans (also known as multi-beneficiary plans) are unique in that they allow more than one beneficiary, but there's a catch. Each beneficiary must be under age 21 at the time he is named as a beneficiary, and each beneficiary must be related to the subscriber of the plan by blood or adoption. To sum it up, individual plans allow anyone to be named as beneficiary, while family plans have age and relationship restrictions.

Here's a point worth noting: Under our tax law, you're not considered to be related to yourself by blood or adoption, nor are you related to your spouse in these ways. As a result, you won't be able to set up a family plan for yourself or your spouse if you're the subscriber (not to mention that you must also be under age 21 to be a beneficiary under a family plan). If you want to set up an RESP for yourself or your spouse, you'll have to choose an individual plan. The same applies to your nieces and nephews. You're not considered to be related to them by blood or adoption, so an individual plan is your only option.

35. Can the same person be named as a beneficiary of more than one RESP? Sure. It's quite common to have a particular child named as the beneficiary of more than one plan. In fact, it may be necessary if more than one person is contributing to RESPs for the child. As I said in question 11, no RESP can have more than one subscriber (unless they are spouses, in which case joint subscribers are okay). So if the grandparents want to contribute to an RESP and the parents do too, they will each have to set up their own RESP for the child. The result is that the child could be a beneficiary of more than one plan.

Keep in mind, however, that the total contributions made annually for the child and the lifetime limit for the child cannot exceed $4,000 and $42,000 respectively, taking into account the combined contributions of all plans for the child.

36. Can I set up an RESP with more than one beneficiary? It's possible to set up a family plan with more than one beneficiary. Under a family plan, each beneficiary must be related to the subscriber by blood or adoption. Question 5 talks about who is considered related to you by blood or adoption, but essentially it is a child, grandchild, great-grandchild, or a sister or brother. Keep in mind that under a family plan each beneficiary must be under age 21 at the time she is named beneficiary.

37. Can I change the beneficiary of the RESP? In most cases, you won't have a problem changing the beneficiary of an RESP, although it could depend on the terms of the specific RESP to which you've subscribed. Check with your RESP promoter first. (In the past, some group plans would not allow a change in beneficiary, but they may have changed their terms.) From a tax point of view, there is generally no problem in changing a beneficiary, although you should keep in mind the rules relating to the following three situations:

- *Over-contributions.* If you name a new beneficiary, all contributions made to the plan over the years for the former beneficiary are deemed to have been made for the new beneficiary, at the time those contributions were actually made. The RESP contribution limits are tracked on a "per beneficiary" basis. The result? If the new beneficiary is already an RESP beneficiary under a different plan, a large over-contribution penalty could arise, especially if maximum contributions have been made to both plans over the years. (See also question 25.)

- *Family plans.* In a family plan, you can replace one beneficiary with another, but only if the new beneficiary is under age 21 and related to the subscriber by blood or adoption. There's some good news here, however. When you replace one beneficiary with another under a family plan, you can say goodbye to any potential over-contribution problem. That's right, Revenue Canada has said that so long as the new beneficiary meets the age and relationship criteria, the deemed contributions I referred to in the paragraph above will not be considered over-contributions.

- *Canada Education Savings Grant (CESG) repayments.* When you change the beneficiary of an RESP, the general rule is that you have to repay the CESGs paid into the plan for the former beneficiary. There is an exception to this rule, however. If the new beneficiary is under age 21 and either a brother or sister of the former beneficiary, or if both beneficiaries are related to the subscriber by blood or adoption, then the CESG payments may not be lost. Keep in mind, however, that there is a restriction on how much in CESGs any one child can receive from the RESP (it's $7,200).

38. Can an RESP family plan be established with cousins as beneficiaries? Cousins qualify as beneficiaries under a family plan only if the subscriber is a grandparent (or great-grandparent). Any other subscriber would have to open individual RESPs for each beneficiary. Under our tax law, an aunt or uncle is not considered related by blood or adoption to a niece or nephew, while a grandparent is.

39. *Does the beneficiary have to maintain a certain grade-point average in school?* Not to worry. There are no requirements for your child to maintain a certain grade-point average to be eligible for educational assistance payments (EAPs) from an RESP, or to receive CESGs out of the plan. To be eligible to receive EAPs, however, a beneficiary must continue to be considered a full-time student at the postsecondary institution at which he is enrolled. In addition, an RESP promoter may impose specific standards for eligibility. As a subscriber, you should consult with your RESP promoter on this matter.

40. *What happens if a beneficiary of an RESP dies before attending a postsecondary school?* The answer depends on whether the RESP is an individual plan or a family plan. In the case of an individual plan, if the beneficiary dies, the subscriber can name anyone else as the beneficiary of the plan (see question 37). If a new beneficiary is not named, the full value of the RESP reverts to the subscriber. If the subscriber has sufficient RRSP contribution room, she can contribute a maximum of $50,000 of the RESP's income to her RRSP. Any excess income not contributed to the RRSP is taxed in the subscriber's hands at her normal marginal rate, and then a 20 percent penalty tax is also applied.

If the RESP is a family plan, it can have multiple beneficiaries so long as all of the beneficiaries are related to the subscriber by blood or adoption and are under age 21 when named as a beneficiary. The benefit of having more than one beneficiary is that educational assistance payments can be allocated to any beneficiary in any manner. If one beneficiary does not pursue a postsecondary education, as would be the case if that beneficiary were to die, then the assets in the plan would be used for the other beneficiaries.

Withdrawals

41. What kind of withdrawals can be made from an RESP?
When you pull money out of an RESP, the withdrawal is classified
as one of four things:

- a tax-free refund of the subscriber's contributions to the plan, called a
  refund of payments
- educational assistance payments (EAPs), which are payments of the
  accumulated income in the plan to the beneficiary for educational
  purposes
- accumulated income payments (AIPs), which are a return to the subscriber of the accumulated income in the plan (usually when none of
  the beneficiaries are pursuing an education)
- a transfer from one plan to another, which can normally take place on
  a tax-free basis. (See question 4 for more on transfers, and Tip 38 in
  Chapter 5 for more information on the various kinds of withdrawals.)

**42. Do the withdrawals from an RESP have to be used for specific
expenses?** No. While it's true that your child must be enrolled in a
qualifying educational program at a postsecondary school before
she can make withdrawals, there is no requirement to account for
how the funds are spent. Having said this, the Department of
Finance intends for students to use the funds for educational
purposes—not to, say, travel the world.

43. Can the RESP subscriber take back his capital at any time?
A withdrawal of the capital contributions to an RESP is called a
refund of payments. Generally, an RESP promoter will allow the
subscriber to take a refund of payments at any time. Some
restrictions may apply, particularly with group plans, but they will
vary from one plan to the next. Be sure to speak with your RESP
promoter about your plan.

44. How are withdrawals from an RESP taxed? The tax implications
of a withdrawal depend on the type of withdrawal. Refunds of

payments and transfers are usually tax-free, while EAPs and AIPs are taxable in the hands of the beneficiary and subscriber respectively. (See Tip 38 in Chapter 5.)

45. How are EAPs made to the beneficiary? EAPs are given to a beneficiary of an RESP once he has enrolled in a qualifying educational program in a postsecondary educational institution—that is, he is

- studying on a full-time basis
- taking courses that are at least three consecutive weeks in length (or more under many group plans—see below)
- spending at least 10 hours per week on the courses or work in the program.

Exceptions are made when the student is disabled.

I should mention here that in the case of group RESPs there may be an additional requirement, imposed by the promoter, for the child to enroll in a program of at least two years' duration. Self-directed plans don't generally have this additional requirement.

If contributions made to the RESP qualified for Canada Education Savings Grants (CESGs), the EAPs will be a combination of accumulated income and CESG deposits. The CESG component will be based on the ratio of CESG funds paid into the plan to the total investment earnings in the plan. Beneficiaries will receive T4A Supplementary slips for the EAPs they receive. When the student reports this income on his tax return, he has a good chance that little or no tax will be due, thanks to the basic personal, tuition, and education credits available to him.

By the way, EAPs are not considered scholarship payments for purposes of the government's $500 scholarship exemption.

46. At what age can a beneficiary begin receiving EAPs?

No restrictions govern the age at which a beneficiary can begin to receive EAPs. To be eligible for EAPs, however, the beneficiary must be enrolled as a full-time student in a qualifying educational program at a postsecondary institution. (See also question 45.)

47. If the RESP has several beneficiaries, do the payments have to be allocated equally among them? For there to be more than one beneficiary of an RESP, it has to be a family plan. EAPs paid out of a family plan RESP can be allocated in any manner to the beneficiaries of the plan—that is, there is no requirement to allocate the accumulated income in the plan to the beneficiaries in equal proportions. (See also question 32.)

48. Can the beneficiary withdraw the RESP assets all at once, or must these withdrawals take place over time? The most that can be withdrawn in the form of EAPs from an RESP in the first 13 weeks of the student's studies is $5,000. After the first 13 weeks, no restrictions apply, provided the beneficiary otherwise qualifies to receive the EAPs (see question 45). Note that the federal Minister of Human Resources Development has the authority to approve an EAP exceeding $5,000 in the first 13 weeks of study on a case-by-case basis. But don't count on getting very far with such a request. Because the 13-week limit covers such a short period, it's likely that the minister will approve a greater amount only in exceptional cases, such as where the cost of tuition for a particular program is substantially higher than average.

One other government-imposed restriction could apply to taking EAPs from an RESP. Where the course taken is less than three months in duration, the maximum EAP that may be taken is the cost of tuition plus $300 per week of study. Again, appeals can also be made to the Minister of Human Resources Development to increase the amount, and the appeals will be considered on a case-by-case basis.

As a final point, be aware that RESP promoters may impose other restrictions related to EAPs, so be sure to consult with your promoter and obtain specific information about your plan.

49. If the RESP beneficiary decides not to pursue an education, what happens to the RESP assets? If your child chooses not to enroll at a postsecondary educational institution, you still have some options to avoid losing the accumulated income in the plan.

Keep in mind that my suggestions here are based on the assumption that they are allowed under the specific terms of your RESP. Be sure to check with your RESP promoter for the terms of your plan.

If we assume that your child does not pursue a postsecondary education, the following alternatives are available to you:

- name a new beneficiary (see question 37)
- allocate the accumulated income to the remaining beneficiaries in the plan
- transfer the assets to a new RESP with other beneficiaries (See Question 4)
- donate the accumulated income to a college or university
- transfer the accumulated income to your RRSP
- receive the accumulated income as a direct receipt (see question 41, item 3).

Before you can transfer the accumulated income to your RRSP or receive the accumulated income as a direct receipt, you must meet all of the following conditions:

- You must be resident in Canada.
- Each beneficiary in the plan for whom you made contributions must be over 21 years of age and not currently eligible to receive EAPs.
- Your RESP must have been in existence for at least 10 years.

In the case of a mentally impaired student, the tax collector may be willing to waive the "age 21" and "10 year" restrictions.

To transfer the accumulated income to your RRSP: If you qualify to receive accumulated income payments (AIPs) and you have RRSP contribution room, you can transfer the accumulated income to your RRSP or your spouse's RRSP (if you are joint subscribers and if your spouse has enough contribution room). The maximum amount you can transfer is $50,000 for 1999 and later years. Here's how it works: You have to include the AIPs in your income and then claim an RRSP deduction for the amount transferred to your RRSP.

To receive accumulated income directly: The other way to recover the accumulated income in the RESP is to simply receive the funds directly. This may be your only option if you have no RRSP contribution room available or if you're over age 69 and no longer have an RRSP. Whatever your situation, when you receive the AIPs, you'll be subject to regular income tax on the income, *and* a 20 percent penalty tax will also apply.

50. If I transfer assets from an RESP to an RRSP, can I avoid income-tax withholdings on the transfer? Truth be known, your RESP promoter is required to withhold tax on any AIP made to you, the subscriber, unless, as I've described in question 49, it is transferred directly to your RRSP and you have sufficient RRSP contribution room to deduct the contribution in that year. If this is the case, you should complete Form T1171, "Tax Withholding Waiver on Accumulated Income Payments from RESPs," which enables the RESP promoter to transfer the payment directly to your RRSP without having to withhold tax on the amount transferred.

51. Will my RRSP contribution room be affected if I transfer assets from an RESP to my RRSP? AIPs that are rolled over into your RRSP will reduce your available RRSP contribution room in the year in which the assets are rolled over. The AIPs are included in your income in the year the funds are rolled out of the RESP and into the RRSP. Offsetting that extra income is the tax deduction to which you're entitled for making a contribution to your RRSP.

Don't forget, this RRSP contribution is going to use up unused RRSP contribution room. The most that can be rolled from an RESP to an RRSP is $50,000. That's a lot of RRSP room to use up all at once.

52. What if my child wants to delay pursuing a postsecondary education? Not to worry. Withdrawals can be deferred up to the end of the year in which the 25th anniversary of the RESP falls. If your child doesn't pursue a postsecondary education by that time, you'll be able to take back your original contributions as a tax-free refund of payments, and the accumulated income as AIPs, but you'll face tax and the 20 percent penalty on the AIPs unless they can be rolled over to your RRSP.

53. What happens if my child decides to transfer to a foreign university? I've got good news and bad news for you. The good news? Your child will be eligible to receive educational assistance payments (EAPs), provided that the course is at least 13 weeks in length and leads to a degree. The bad news? Your child's residency for tax purposes is pretty important here. You see, EAPs paid to a non-resident can't include accumulated CESGs. This means that as your non-resident child receives money out of the RESP, the accumulated income balance will be depleted while accumulated CESGs will remain in the plan. If the accumulated CESGs are still in the RESP when all the investment income has been paid out and the plan is terminated, the accumulated CESGs must be repaid to the government.

But keep this in mind: In many cases, a student attending a foreign college or university does not give up residency (for tax purposes) because she plans to return to Canada when her schooling is complete. Whether a person is deemed to have given up Canadian residency or not is determined by the specifics of the situation, including the individual's intention at the time of the move, her personal and social ties to Canada, her ties to the foreign country, and the length and frequency of her visits back to Canada. It may be a good idea for your child to maintain Canadian residency until all EAPs have been received from the RESP, just to avoid repaying the CESG money.

54. Are correspondence courses eligible for EAPs? Since 1997, students who enroll in full-time correspondence courses and who are otherwise eligible can receive EAPs from an RESP—assuming, of course, that the terms of the individual plan allow it.

55. Can EAPs be withdrawn from an RESP when the student receives scholarships or when the student's education is otherwise subsidized? Look at it this way, if your child doesn't have any approved postsecondary education costs (assuming the scholarship covers all normal costs), then no EAPs would be available. But in most cases scholarships and other "free" money will cover only part (and usually a small part!) of the costs of education. As a result, the student will not usually have a problem withdrawing EAPs.

Canada Education Savings Grants

56. What are Canada Education Savings Grants? In the last few years, the need to take measures to reduce deficits has dictated that governments at all levels can no longer fund postsecondary education to the extent they used to fund it. As a result, those who want a postsecondary education and their families have to come up with a larger proportion of costs. The federal government's position is that it will partner with parents, grandparents, and other family members or friends of children to help them save for the postsecondary education of these children. To this end, the government introduced in its 1998 federal budget the Canada Education Savings Grant (CESG).

The CESG, which is available to qualifying students, is a grant that is deposited directly into an RESP to supplement the contributions being made by the plan's subscriber. The grant is worth 20 percent of the contributions made by the subscriber, to a maximum of $400 for each year. This maximum $400 CESG is deposited into the plan when $2,000 (20% X $2,000 = $400) for each year is contributed to an RESP for an eligible child.

57. Who qualifies for the CESG? Every child who is a resident of Canada is eligible to receive CESGs for contributions made to an RESP after 1997. Here's how it works: Beginning in 1998, each child will accumulate CESG room of $2,000 each year, up to and including the year in which he turns age 17. The CESG is payable on contributions made to an RESP, but only as long as the child has CESG room. If you don't use up the CESG room available in a year by making sufficient contributions to an RESP, the unused room can be carried forward for use in the future.

Special rules apply to kids who are age 16 or 17. To encourage the use of RESPs, the government has said that kids who attain age 16 or 17 in the year will receive a CESG only where one of the following conditions applies:

- a minimum of $2,000 of RESP contributions was made for the beneficiary before the year in which the beneficiary reached age 16, *or*
- a minimum of $100 in annual RESP contributions was made for the beneficiary in any of the four years before the year in which the beneficiary reached age 16.

In addition, as a transitional measure, a child who turned 16 or 17 in 1998 is deemed eligible for the CESG if he was a named beneficiary of an RESP during any of the four years before 1998.

58. *Is there a limit on how much in CESGs a child can receive in a lifetime?* There sure is. Your child is entitled to receive a maximum of $7,200 in CESG funds ($400 per year for 18 years) paid out of an RESP for her benefit. On top of the grant money, your child can keep all of the income accumulated by the grants.

59. *Are the CESG payments paid per beneficiary, or per RESP account?* The CESG payments are made by the government for each beneficiary, not for each RESP. If, for example, you set up a family plan with three eligible beneficiaries, a total of $1,200 ($400 per beneficiary) in CESGs can be paid into that one RESP each year, assuming you make the necessary contributions to the plan.

60. *When and how are the CESG payments made?* CESG payments look like this: The RESP promoter you have chosen applies for the CESG on your behalf. (The promoter will require a social insurance number for the beneficiary before applying for the CESG.) Human Resources Development Canada processes CESG applications and calculates the CESG. The appropriate CESG is

then issued to the trustee. The trustee deposits the CESG payment into your RESP account to be invested as per your instructions.

The grants are paid on a quarterly basis. If you make an RESP contribution before March 31, the CESG will be paid to your RESP by the end of April. The other cutoff dates are June 30, September 30, and December 31. If RESP contributions are made by these dates, the CESG will be paid to your RESP by the end of the following month.

61. Does the CESG payment reduce the amount I can contribute to the RESP? Absolutely not. Any CESG payments made to your RESP are made over and above the $4,000 annual and $42,000 lifetime limits imposed for each beneficiary.

62. How is the CESG money paid out of the RESP to my child? When your child enrolls in a postsecondary program at a school that qualifies under the terms of the *Income Tax Act* as well the terms of the RESP plan to which you've subscribed, your child is eligible to receive the CESG. When an educational assistance payment (EAP) is withdrawn from the RESP, it can consist of two components: the accumulated income in the RESP (including the accumulated income on the CESGs), and the CESGs themselves. The CESG portion of the EAP is based on the ratio of CESGs paid into the plan to total investment earnings in the plan, and it reduces the remaining balance in the plan's CESG "account."

For example, if the total accumulated income in the RESP (including the income that has accumulated on the CESG funds over the years) amounts to $40,000, and the total CESG funds in the plan amount to $7,200, then 18 percent ($7,200 out of $40,000) of each EAP is considered a payment of the CESGs to the child for educational purposes. If $10,000 is paid out as EAPs in the first year of schooling, $1,800 of it is considered CESG money. That would leave just $5,400 ($7,200 minus $1,800) of CESG money in the plan after the first year.

63. In what type of education program must my child enroll?

In question 45, I talked about the requirements that have to be met to receive EAPs. In order to receive CESGs out of the RESP, your child must meet the criteria to receive EAPs, in general. To recap, the course must be at a postsecondary level and it must last at least three weeks and include 10 hours of instruction each week. Outside Canada, the course must last 13 weeks and be at a postsecondary level. EAPs are limited to the cost of tuition plus $300 per week if the course is less than three months in duration.

64. What if my child's RESP has received the grant but my child does not pursue postsecondary education?

If your child does not enroll in a qualifying educational program, you have to repay the original grant amounts. You *can* keep the income earned on the CESGs, however. Some other situations could give rise to repayments of CESGs (see question 65).

65. When must the CESGs be repaid?

There are five situations in which you may have to repay the CESG funds that were paid into your child's RESP (see Tip 49 in Chapter 5 for details):

- when contributions are withdrawn for non-educational purposes
- when the accumulated income in the plan is withdrawn for non-educational purposes
- when the plan is terminated or revoked
- when a beneficiary under a plan is replaced (with some exceptions)
- when certain transfers are made from one RESP to another.

You'll be interested to know that your RESP promoter is prohibited from making a refund of contributions or a payment of RESP accumulated income for non-educational purposes that would deplete the assets of the RESP so much that it would make repayment of the CESGs impossible.

Here's one last point, related to group plans: The requirement to repay CESG money when a beneficiary does not pursue an education does not generally apply to group plans, which operate on the basis of age cohorts, provided the CESG money is reallocated to other

RESPs in the group arrangement. The $7,200 limit on the amount of CESG money that can be paid out for any one beneficiary in the group plan still applies.

66. Is it possible to lose CESG room? Sure it is. Any withdrawal of unassisted contributions (that is, contributions that have not generated CESGs) made after February 23, 1998, from an RESP for non-educational purposes causes restrictions to be put on future CESG payments for the beneficiaries of that plan. (See Tip 50 in Chapter 5.)

67. If I don't contribute $2,000 to an RESP each year, can I carry forward the unused CESG room? Yes, you can carry forward any unused CESG contribution room from a previous year to be used in the future. For example, you could contribute $1,000 this year and get $200 in CESGs, then contribute $3,000 next year and get $600. In this case, you've "caught up" your usage of the CESG room. But before you decide to skip RESP contributions and carry forward the CESG room, keep in mind that the maximum contribution you're entitled to make to an RESP is $4,000 each year. As a result, allowing your CESG room to build up significantly could result in your being unable to make large enough contributions to the RESP to catch up and use the available CESG room. Not to mention that you'll lose some tax-free compounding of investment returns inside the RESP by deferring contributions to the plan.

68. Can I carry forward excess contributions to claim a CESG in a future year? Sorry, but if your contribution is greater than the amount needed to receive the maximum available CESG, you can't carry the excess contribution forward to another year and use it to claim CESGs. For example, if you contribute $4,000 to an RESP this year, you can't use $2,000 to claim a $400 grant this year and the remaining $2,000 next year to claim another $400 grant. You'd be better to plan your contributions so that you don't waste them. If, for example, you have $4,000 this year and you're not sure you can contribute another $2,000 next year, you should consider splitting that $4,000 in two and contributing $2,000 this year and the remaining $2,000 next year.

69. Can I obtain CESGs for contributions I made to an RESP before the grant was introduced? No, you can't. These are considered "unassisted" contributions, and special rules are in place to ensure that you don't recycle these contributions to obtain CESG payments on them (see question 66).

70. I opened an RESP several years ago. Will future contributions to this RESP be eligible for the CESG? Contributions to plans in existence before 1998 qualify for the CESG where the terms of those plans are amended prior to 2000. Check with your RESP promoter to make sure the appropriate changes are made. These changes include the following:

- In the case of a family plan, the terms of the plan prohibit the addition of beneficiaries over the age of 21.
- The plan restricts educational assistance payments (EAPs) during the first 13 weeks of a course to $5,000.
- The plan rules state that EAPs paid to a beneficiary will not include accumulated CESG amounts if the individual became a beneficiary after turning 21.

As a transitional measure, contributions made in 1998 or 1999 are eligible for the CESG without the above amendments. But for contributions after 1999, make sure the above changes are made to your RESP. Your RESP promoter should be on the ball enough to make these changes, but if you're not sure the changes have been made, it may make sense to open a new RESP, which will already meet the conditions above.

71. If only one child enrolls in a qualifying educational program, can that child receive all of the CESGs in the plan as EAPs? It may be possible to use some of the CESGs that were paid into your RESP for one child for the benefit of another child who is also a beneficiary under the plan. The overriding rule here is that the total amount of CESGs paid out of the RESP to the beneficiary as EAPs cannot exceed the child's lifetime maximum of $7,200. For example, if a total of $10,000 in CESGs has been contributed to the RESP for two children (assume $5,000 each), and one child does not enroll in a qualifying program of study, the second child could take his own $5,000 in CESGs plus another $2,200 of the other child's CESGs, bringing the total CESG amounts for the child pursuing education to $7,200. The balance of the CESG funds would be repaid to the government.

72. Is it necessary to open an RESP today to earn CESG contribution room? No. Beginning in 1998, each child who is a resident of Canada and who was age 17 or under in that year began to accumulate CESG contribution room, regardless of whether or not the child is named as a beneficiary under an RESP. For example, if a child is born in 1998 but no RESP is opened for the child until 2001, the child will have accumulated a total of $8,000 ($2,000 per year for 4 years) in CESG room by 2001.

73. If one beneficiary is named under two plans, and contributions are made to each plan, which plan gets the CESG? The CESG is paid on a first-come, first-served basis, subject to annual and lifetime limits. In the event that two subscribers make contributions in the same quarter to two separate RESPs, the subscriber's contribution dated earliest in the quarter will receive the CESG. In the event that the contributions are made on the same day, the grant will be pro-rated.

74. Are any fees applied to the CESG? Nope. There are no fees associated with the CESG, although some RESP promoters may apply service or administration fees. If so, those fees would depend on the RESP promoter and the RESP contract signed by the subscriber. Make sure you understand the fees being charged by your plan!

75. *If the CESG has to be repaid and the investment has dropped in value, what happens?* Losses are considered to come first from your contributions and last from the CESG funds deposited in the plan. If the total value of a plan at a particular time is less than the amount of the CESGs received, then the RESP promoter is prohibited from returning any contributions to you as the subscriber. Under these circumstances only EAPs would be permitted.

Here's an example. Suppose you contributed $40,000 over the lifetime of the RESP for your child. The government has kicked in an additional $7,200 in CESGs, for total contributions of $47,200. The value of the plan today is just $20,000. The losses incurred are applied first to the contributions you made, so the government's CESG money is still intact. If the grants have to be repaid, the CESG funds are still in the plan and can be repaid. The value of the RESP would have to fall below $7,200 before the government loses anything. The RESP promoter is prohibited from making any payments out of the plan for non-educational purposes if this will make it impossible to repay the full amount of the CESG from the plan assets.

76. *Can a beneficiary receive more than one CESG deposit to a plan per year?* Sure, but the CESG payments in total must not exceed the annual limit of $400 ($800 if sufficient accumulated CESG room exists) and the lifetime limit of $7,200.

77. *Can a subscriber catch up on lost CESGs if she obtained a social insurance number (SIN) for the child in a later year?* CESG contribution room begins to accumulate from whichever is later: when a child is born or January 1, 1998. Whether or not the child has a SIN, grant room accumulates at $2,000 per year per beneficiary. Because of the $4,000 annual RESP contribution limits, however, no beneficiary can receive grants exceeding $800 (20 percent of $4,000) in one calendar year. The purpose of the SIN is simply to allow Human Resources Development Canada to track how much in CESGs have been paid for each child. As a

result, it's possible to contribute to an RESP to entitle your child to CESGs even when your child doesn't have a SIN, but no CESGs will be paid into the RESP until a SIN is provided.

78. **Can a beneficiary of an RESP who has given up Canadian residency remain eligible for the CESG?** No chance. To be eligible for the CESG, the beneficiary must be a resident of Canada for tax purposes. Whether a person is resident in Canada for tax purposes is a complex matter. Contact a tax pro if you have any questions about residency. CESG money accumulated in the RESP up to the date of departure remains in the plan, but the beneficiary will not accumulate grant contribution room while she is not a resident of Canada. Upon her return to Canada, the accumulation of grant room will resume.

79. **Will my child lose the CESG previously paid into the plan if he gives up Canadian residency?** The CESG money will remain in the RESP until EAPs are made or the plan is closed. If the beneficiary is not considered a resident of Canada at the time EAPs are paid, he will not be entitled to the CESG. That is, the EAPs paid out will consist only of accumulated income (including income on the CESGs), but not CESG capital. If the child completes postsecondary education and CESG money is still sitting in the plan, it will have to be repaid to the government.

Investments

80. **When should I start investing for my child's education?** The effects of compound investment returns make it much more advantageous to start saving for your child's education when she is very young. Consider a parent who sets aside $4,000 annually from the time his child is born, until the child reaches age 10, for total contributions of $40,000 ($4,000 each year for 10 years), and then allows that $40,000 to grow until the child is age 18. When

combined with the Canada Education Savings Grants (CESGs) available from the government, the total available to the child at age 18 will be $127,419 (assuming an 8 percent annual rate of return).

Now assume that same parent invests the same $40,000 over 10 years, but waits until his child is age 5 to start investing. When the child is age 18, she will have available to her just $86,719—a full $40,700 less—just because the investment program started 5 years later. If you haven't started a savings program yet, you've lost time, but it's always better to start late than never.

81. *What investments can I hold in my RESP?* As part of the draft budget legislation released on October 27, 1998, the government introduced new rules dealing with qualified investments for RESPs. The rules pretty much mirror the rules surrounding qualifying investments for RRSPs. (See Tip 44 in Chapter 5 for a list of qualifying investments.)

82. *What happens to non-qualifying investments in an RESP that were made before the new rules?* The good news is that all property acquired by your RESP on or before October 27, 1998, is considered to be a qualifying investment for the RESP, even if the investment would not qualify after that date. But if you dispose of this property, it can't be reacquired later since it is a non-qualifying investment currently.

83. *Is it true that the foreign content rules for an RESP are different from the rules for an RRSP?* Unlike your RRSP, where foreign content is limited to 20 percent of the book value of the plan, there's no limit to the amount of foreign property you can hold in an RESP. If you're smart, you'll take full advantage of this fact and heavily weight your RESP investments to foreign content. After all, foreign equities have typically outperformed Canadian equities over the long run. (See Tip 27 in Chapter 3.)

84. *Can I buy investments in an RESP on margin?* Nope. The draft legislation released on October 27, 1998, clarified that an RESP's

registration becomes revocable when the plan holds a non-qualifying investment, borrows money, or operates a business. Buying on margin qualifies as borrowing money. The plan could lose its registered status—and you don't want that. It could result in your being required to repay CESGs in the plan and to pay tax on any income accumulated to date in the plan, along with a 20 percent penalty on that income.

85. Is there a chance I could lose my invested capital in an RESP? The risk of losing money in an RESP is no greater than the risk of losing money by investing outside an RESP. It's a function of the types of investments you hold, and really has nothing to do with the terms or nature of an RESP itself. (Some very old group RESPs, however, may still require you to forfeit the accumulated income on your contributions if your child does not enroll in a qualifying educational program.) In many cases today, the investment of choice inside an RESP is mutual funds. And for the most part, you can't go wrong over the long term with equity mutual funds as the core of your RESP portfolio. Provided you're not buying exclusively high-risk stocks in a self-directed RESP, it would be tough to lose money over the long term. Your main concern should be to generate a return sufficient to grow the RESP assets to what they need to be down the road when your child goes to school. If you're not sure how to do this, I highly recommend that you seek the help of a competent financial adviser.

In-Trust Accounts

86. Is it possible to transfer assets from an in-trust account to an RESP? This is generally a no-no. Using the assets of an in-trust account to subscribe to an RESP could be a violation of provincial trust law. You see, under provincial trust law, if no trust indenture (agreement) exists—which is the case with an in-trust account—then no provision exists to change the nature of the trust. The trustee is obligated to simply hold the assets for the benefit of the beneficiary until the beneficiary requests a distribution of the assets of the trust (which can take place once the child reaches the age of majority).

Transferring the assets of an in-trust account to an RESP would clearly change the nature of an existing trust. After all, the subscriber to an RESP has the ability to take back her contributions, which is not possible with an in-trust account. Any trustee transferring the assets of an in-trust account to an RESP could be held accountable for doing so if the beneficiary decided to pursue legal action, however unlikely that seems.

In addition, the subscriber to an RESP cannot be a trust. If an in-trust account is considered to be a legal trust (as most lawyers would agree), then a transfer from an in-trust account is not allowed under our tax law.

87. *If I'm the contributor to the in-trust account, can I also be the trustee?* Yes, but it's a bad idea. You see, your intention when you set up the in-trust account was to ensure that your child (the beneficiary) pays tax on the capital gains earned in the account—not you. Naming yourself as trustee when you are also the contributor could throw a wrench into this income-splitting strategy. And it's all because of subsection 75(2) of our tax law. That little subsection says that whenever a person transfers property to a trust (which you have done as contributor) and then maintains control over the dispositions of the property in the trust (which you would do by also being the trustee), that person will pay tax on all the income of the trust, including capital gains. That's right, your child would pay no tax whatsoever on the earnings in the account. You would pay all the tax—which really defeats the purpose of the account. Revenue Canada is generally satisfied if you name your spouse or another individual as trustee of an account to which you are the contributor.

88. Is it necessary to file a tax return for an in-trust account?
Technically speaking, you're supposed to file a tax and
information return for a trust each year. But it's the practice of
Revenue Canada not to require this tax and information return
where the total income of the trust is less than $500 and the
income payable to any particular beneficiary is less than $100.
This practice could get a number of in-trust accounts off the hook
when it comes to tax-filing time. The problem is that many in-trust
accounts are growing in size, and could fall into the requirement
to file annually. Revenue Canada has not enforced the filing
requirement for in-trust accounts in the past (regardless of the
amount in the account or the income generated), but this could
change since the tax dollars at stake are growing annually.

**89. Do I have to file a tax return for my child who has earned
capital gains in the in-trust account?** There are certain situations
where you're required to file a tax return. One of these situations
arises when a taxpayer has capital gains to report. If you choose
not to file a tax return for a child who has earned capital gains in
the in-trust account, what are the consequences? Penalties could be
levied. Funny enough, the penalties are based on the amount of
tax owing on the tax return. If your child's capital gains, along
with his other income, are low enough not to trigger any tax, then
the penalty owing will be nil. The bottom line? Technically you're
supposed to file, but there won't be any penalty if you don't—
provided your child's income is low enough not to trigger any tax.

**90. Can I transfer the assets of an in-trust account to a formal trust
later?** Sorry, but generally you can't do this. I'm going to refer you to
my answer to question 86. The reasoning is the same here. An in-
trust account is really a bare trust, and the trustee does not have the
authority to change its terms. Moving to a formal trust would change
the nature and terms of the trust, which could be a violation of
provincial trust law. From a practical point of view, unless the
beneficiaries of the in-trust account take some exception to the

transfer, you're not likely to run into any problems, but you do need to recognize that you could be in violation of trust law just the same.

I should mention that it may be possible to argue that an in-trust account is really not a trust at all, and therefore provincial trust law has no authority over it, but this issue is far from clear. You'll want to consult a lawyer experienced in trusts if you're seriously considering the transfer of sizeable assets from an in-trust account to a formal trust.

91. Which is better for education savings—an RESP or an in-trust account? You know, I prefer not to think of RESPs and in-trust accounts as fierce competitors for your education savings dollar. I think there's a place for both in every education savings strategy. I do recommend that, as a minimum, you contribute $2,000 annually to an RESP to take advantage of the CESG payments, but beyond this, you'll likely reach your education savings goals regardless of whether you choose an RESP or an in-trust account for your child's education fund.

Determining which vehicle to use to set aside education funds depends partly on how much time you have before your child heads to school. If your child has fewer than 10 years to go, you may be hard-pressed to set aside enough in an RESP due to the $4,000 maximum annual contribution limit. In this case, you may have no choice but to make use of an in-trust account as well, although taking advantage of the CESG payments to the extent possible makes lots of sense. To give you some idea of the way the two vehicles compare, I've provided a table that begins on the following page.

92. Will in-trust accounts set up in the names of my children qualify for the CESG? I'm afraid not. A child's in-trust account is not included in the CESG program. Interestingly, my observation has been that children are much more likely to go on to higher education if an RESP has been set up for them. Perhaps this is the reason the government wants to encourage parents to save through RESPs. If the Department of Finance had simply wanted to put

TAKE YOUR PICK: REGISTERED EDUCATION SAVINGS PLANS OR IN–TRUST ACCOUNTS

	Registered Education Savings Plans	In–trust Accounts
Contribution limits	$4,000 per beneficiary per year. Lifetime maximum of $42,000 per beneficiary.	No limit.
Investment options	No restrictions under a self–directed plan. Investment or savings account plans generally offer one type of savings vehicle or mutual fund family. Group plans generally offer no options.	Generally no restrictions, although some have expressed concern due to provincial trustee legislation. These concerns will likely be put to rest over time.
Government assistance	Canada Education Savings Grant. The grant is 20% of contributions made within the child's grant room—normally a maximum of $400 annually.	None.
Control over assets	The subscriber controls the investments and decides when to pay the assets to the beneficiary.	The trustee of the account controls where the money is invested. The assets, however, must be held for the child until age of majority; then the assets revert to the child.
Use of assets	A beneficiary must use the plan assets for post–secondary education;	Child may use the assets for any purpose once reaching age of majority. Contributor

Continues

Continued

	Registered Education Savings Plans	In–trust Accounts
	otherwise, assets revert to the subscriber. If assets revert to subscriber, income tax plus a 20% penalty will be due on the accumulated income in the plan, unless the assets are transferred to the subscriber's RRSP.	may not use the assets in any way, since the assets belong to the child.
Recovery of capital	Subscribers may receive a tax–free return of original capital at any time. Certain trustee or administration fees may apply.	Contributor has no right to recover the assets in the account since the assets belong to the child.
Taxation of assets	Assets grow tax–deferred over the years. When student withdraws this money to attend a qualifying educational program, student will pay tax on accumulated income in the plan.	Interest and dividends are taxed in the hands of the contributor annually. Realized capital gains are taxed in the hands of the child annually.
Tax filings	No annual filings are required until the student makes withdrawals from the RESP. Then student must file returns to report the taxable income.	Must file a tax return for the child to report capital gains. Technically, a trust tax return should be filed annually, but Revenue Canada has not, to date, been enforcing these filings for in–trust accounts.

money into the hands of kids for the future, they likely would have favoured in-trust accounts as well.

93. Is it possible with an in-trust account to pay the assets to the child over the course of her postsecondary school years, rather than all at once at the age of majority? There are no tax implications to transferring the in-trust account assets to the beneficiary, since those assets are beneficially owned by the child already. However, under provincial trust law, there's a non-tax consequence to the beneficiary of a bare trust (such as an in-trust account) achieving the age of majority. The trustee no longer has the right to withhold the assets from the beneficiary since the beneficiary has a right to the assets at that point (there is no trust document to say any different). In fact, the beneficiary can demand that the funds be handed over, and the trustee has no recourse. All of this, of course, assumes that an in-trust account is a legal trust, which is the general consensus among lawyers.

94. What are the approximate set-up costs and annual expenses for a formal trust and an informal trust account? Setting up a formal trust involves legal documentation, in the form of a trust indenture, or agreement. The cost can vary according to the agreement's complexity. Generally, you can expect the cost of legal fees to fall between $1,000 and $3,000. An informal in-trust account usually has no set-up costs. But beware, you may be getting what you pay for. A formal trust provides a greater degree of control and certainty than an in-trust account. Talk to a lawyer familiar with trust law in your province for a quote on setting up a formal trust, and to discuss the pros and cons.

95. How can I ensure my child uses the money in an in-trust account for an education? In short, you can't. The assets in the in-trust account belong to the child, who has a right to take possession of those assets once he reaches the age of majority. If your child wants to spend the money on a new car stereo, a trip to

Aruba, or penny stocks, you can't do much about it. Your best bet would be to teach your child from a young age that the money sitting in the account is intended for an education. You might even impose some type of sanction if the funds aren't used for that purpose. It's up to you. Best of luck!

96. *Is there a way to avoid the attribution rules on income from an in-trust account?* I suspect it's no secret to you that capital gains realized in an in-trust account are generally taxable in the beneficiary's hands. It's the interest and dividend income that can pose a problem. Under the attribution rules, any interest or dividends earned in the account are taxable in the hands of the person who contributed the money to the account. The good news is that the attribution rules only apply to first-generation income. Second-generation income (income on income) is not attributed to the contributor. So, here's your game plan: Transfer any interest and dividends earned each year to a separate investment account in the name of your child. This income will grow free of the attribution rules, while only the capital sitting in the first account will face these rules annually.

97. *What are the implications if an in-trust account is a real trust?* There is some debate about whether an in-trust account is really a trust or not. If the account is a real trust, then it will be what's known as a "bare" trust. Under a bare trust, the trustee has virtually no authority other than to hold the assets for the beneficiary until the beneficiary demands that the assets be distributed to her.

Implications exist under both tax law and trust law if an in-trust account is really a trust. Subsection 75(2) of our tax law applies to trusts. This provision is an attribution rule that will tax you—the person transferring property to the trust—on all income earned in the trust if any of the following conditions apply:
- the trust property can revert to you
- you're able to name or change beneficiaries after the trust is set up, *or*
- the property can be disposed of only with your consent or direction.

Then, of course, there's the requirement to file a trust tax and information return. Under provincial trust law, you lack the authority to do anything with the assets in the trust other than invest them and hold them for the child's taking at age of majority. In the absence of a trust agreement, trust law also restricts the types of investments that can be held in the trust. In some provinces, mutual funds do not make it to the list of permissible investments (although this situation is likely to change very soon).

If an in-trust account is *not* a valid trust arrangement, you'll avoid some of the headaches I've just mentioned (since certain provisions in tax and trust law will no longer apply to the account).

98. Should I open a separate in-trust account for each child, or just one for all my kids? Your best bet is to open a separate account for each child. You won't face much additional cost, if any, in doing this, and it will allow you to split the assets among the kids as you see fit. If the kids are named as beneficiaries on the same in-trust account, they would have to split the assets in the account proportionately. This may not be ideal if your kids are different ages and one will need the assets in the account before the others, or if one will need more support from you than the others.

99. Can my spouse and I both be named as trustees on the in-trust account without a problem? I would recommend that one individual who has not made any contributions to the account be named trustee. If this is not practical, then having spouses as joint trustees is likely to pass Revenue Canada's condition of ensuring that the contributor actually has given up ownership and made a true transfer of property to the child. This is not entirely clear, however. Revenue Canada has not written any technical interpretations on this issue, and all we can do is speculate. But I'll tell you what, if you try this idea and are reassessed by the tax collector, let me know. I'll update my answer to this question. I don't have a good gut feeling about the strategy though.

WINNING THE EDUCATION SAVINGS GAME

If you hope to win the education savings game, you have to get answers to your questions, especially those that relate to RESPs and CESGs. I've gone to great lengths in this chapter to answer every conceivable question you could have. I've even dealt with the most common questions about in-trust accounts. As I said at the beginning of this chapter, if you come up with the 100th question, one I haven't answered here, just visit The WaterStreet Group's Web site at www.waterstreet.ca and ask your question there in our Tax Talk discussion forum, or in the Mail Bag area of the site. Heck, if you're really having trouble, don't hesitate to call my office and speak to one of our tax professionals. We can be reached at (416) 410-4410, or by e-mail at group@waterstreet.ca. My e-mail address is tim@waterstreet.ca. I'm committed to helping you make the right decisions. If your question takes time to research, we'll have to quote a fee for completing the work, but it doesn't hurt to ask!

APPENDIX A

Estimate of Education Costs—
Tuition Inflation At 5 Percent

Assumed inflation for tuition costs   5.00%
Assumed inflation for other costs   3.00%

LIVING AWAY FROM HOME

Year Start School	Tuition	Books & Supplies	Accommo- dation	Food	Entertain- ment	Transport	Personal Care	Total	Four-Year Total
1999	$3,403	$1,200	$3,200	$1,400	$1,200	$1,000	$1,500	$12,903	$54,412
2000	$3,573	$1,236	$3,296	$1,442	$1,236	$1,030	$1,545	$13,358	$56,338
2001	$3,752	$1,273	$3,395	$1,485	$1,273	$1,061	$1,591	$13,830	$58,336
2002	$3,939	$1,311	$3,497	$1,530	$1,311	$1,093	$1,639	$14,320	$60,409
2003	$4,136	$1,351	$3,602	$1,576	$1,351	$1,126	$1,688	$14,829	$62,561
2004	$4,343	$1,391	$3,710	$1,623	$1,391	$1,159	$1,739	$15,356	$64,794
2005	$4,560	$1,433	$3,821	$1,672	$1,433	$1,194	$1,791	$15,904	$67,113
2006	$4,788	$1,476	$3,936	$1,722	$1,476	$1,230	$1,845	$16,472	$69,519
2007	$5,028	$1,520	$4,054	$1,773	$1,520	$1,267	$1,900	$17,062	$72,017
2008	$5,279	$1,566	$4,175	$1,827	$1,566	$1,305	$1,957	$17,675	$74,611
2009	$5,543	$1,613	$4,301	$1,881	$1,613	$1,344	$2,016	$18,310	$77,305
2010	$5,820	$1,661	$4,430	$1,938	$1,661	$1,384	$2,076	$18,971	$80,102
2011	$6,111	$1,711	$4,562	$1,996	$1,711	$1,426	$2,139	$19,656	$83,007
2012	$6,417	$1,762	$4,699	$2,056	$1,762	$1,469	$2,203	$20,368	$86,024
2013	$6,738	$1,815	$4,840	$2,118	$1,815	$1,513	$2,269	$21,107	$89,157
2014	$7,075	$1,870	$4,985	$2,181	$1,870	$1,558	$2,337	$21,875	$92,413
2015	$7,428	$1,926	$5,135	$2,247	$1,926	$1,605	$2,407	$22,673	$95,795
2016	$7,800	$1,983	$5,289	$2,314	$1,983	$1,653	$2,479	$23,502	$99,309
2017	$8,190	$2,043	$5,448	$2,383	$2,043	$1,702	$2,554	$24,363	$102,961
2018	$8,599	$2,104	$5,611	$2,455	$2,104	$1,754	$2,630	$25,258	$106,756
2019	$9,029	$2,167	$5,780	$2,529	$2,167	$1,806	$2,709	$26,187	$110,700
2020	$9,481	$2,232	$5,953	$2,604	$2,232	$1,860	$2,790	$27,153	$114,799
2021	$9,955	$2,299	$6,132	$2,683	$2,299	$1,916	$2,874	$28,158	$119,060

LIVING AT HOME

Year Start School	Tuition	Books & Supplies	Accommo- dation	Food	Entertain- ment	Transport	Personal Care	Total	Four-Year Total
1999	$3,403	$1,200	$-	$-	$1,200	$500	$1,500	$7,803	$33,075
2000	$3,573	$1,236	$-	$-	$1,236	$515	$1,545	$8,105	$34,361
2001	$3,752	$1,273	$-	$-	$1,273	$530	$1,591	$8,420	$35,700
2002	$3,939	$1,311	$-	$-	$1,311	$546	$1,639	$8,747	$37,094
2003	$4,136	$1,351	$-	$-	$1,351	$563	$1,688	$9,089	$38,547
2004	$4,343	$1,391	$-	$-	$1,391	$580	$1,739	$9,444	$40,060
2005	$4,560	$1,433	$-	$-	$1,433	$597	$1,791	$9,814	$41,636
2006	$4,788	$1,476	$-	$-	$1,476	$615	$1,845	$10,200	$43,278
2007	$5,028	$1,520	$-	$-	$1,520	$633	$1,900	$10,602	$44,989
2008	$5,279	$1,566	$-	$-	$1,566	$652	$1,957	$11,020	$46,772
2009	$5,543	$1,613	$-	$-	$1,613	$672	$2,016	$11,456	$48,630
2010	$5,820	$1,661	$-	$-	$1,661	$692	$2,076	$11,911	$50,567
2011	$6,111	$1,711	$-	$-	$1,711	$713	$2,139	$12,385	$52,586
2012	$6,417	$1,762	$-	$-	$1,762	$734	$2,203	$12,878	$54,690
2013	$6,738	$1,815	$-	$-	$1,815	$756	$2,269	$13,393	$56,884
2014	$7,075	$1,870	$-	$-	$1,870	$779	$2,337	$13,930	$59,171
2015	$7,428	$1,926	$-	$-	$1,926	$802	$2,407	$14,489	$61,556
2016	$7,800	$1,983	$-	$-	$1,983	$826	$2,479	$15,072	$64,043
2017	$8,190	$2,043	$-	$-	$2,043	$851	$2,554	$15,680	$66,637
2018	$8,599	$2,104	$-	$-	$2,104	$877	$2,630	$16,315	$69,342
2019	$9,029	$2,167	$-	$-	$2,167	$903	$2,709	$16,976	$72,164
2020	$9,481	$2,232	$-	$-	$2,232	$930	$2,790	$17,666	$75,107
2021	$9,955	$2,299	$-	$-	$2,299	$958	$2,874	$18,386	$78,177

Estimate of Education Costs—Tuition Inflation At 7 Percent

| Assumed inflation for tuition costs | 7.00% |
| Assumed inflation for other costs | 3.00% |

LIVING AWAY FROM HOME

Year Start School	Tuition	Books & Supplies	Accommo- dation	Food	Entertain- ment	Transport	Personal Care	Total	Four-Year Total
1999	$3,403	$1,200	$3,200	$1,400	$1,200	$1,000	$1,500	$12,903	$54,854
2000	$3,641	$1,236	$3,296	$1,442	$1,236	$1,030	$1,545	$13,426	$57,104
2001	$3,896	$1,273	$3,395	$1,485	$1,273	$1,061	$1,591	$13,975	$59,463
2002	$4,169	$1,311	$3,497	$1,530	$1,311	$1,093	$1,639	$14,550	$61,939
2003	$4,461	$1,351	$3,602	$1,576	$1,351	$1,126	$1,688	$15,153	$64,538
2004	$4,773	$1,391	$3,710	$1,623	$1,391	$1,159	$1,739	$15,786	$67,266
2005	$5,107	$1,433	$3,821	$1,672	$1,433	$1,194	$1,791	$16,450	$70,132
2006	$5,464	$1,476	$3,936	$1,722	$1,476	$1,230	$1,845	$17,148	$73,143
2007	$5,847	$1,520	$4,054	$1,773	$1,520	$1,267	$1,900	$17,881	$76,307
2008	$6,256	$1,566	$4,175	$1,827	$1,566	$1,305	$1,957	$18,652	$79,635
2009	$6,694	$1,613	$4,301	$1,881	$1,613	$1,344	$2,016	$19,461	$83,135
2010	$7,163	$1,661	$4,430	$1,938	$1,661	$1,384	$2,076	$20,313	$86,818
2011	$7,664	$1,711	$4,562	$1,996	$1,711	$1,426	$2,139	$21,209	$90,695
2012	$8,201	$1,762	$4,699	$2,056	$1,762	$1,469	$2,203	$22,152	$94,777
2013	$8,775	$1,815	$4,840	$2,118	$1,815	$1,513	$2,269	$23,144	$99,076
2014	$9,389	$1,870	$4,985	$2,181	$1,870	$1,558	$2,337	$24,190	$103,607
2015	$10,046	$1,926	$5,135	$2,247	$1,926	$1,605	$2,407	$25,291	$108,383
2016	$10,749	$1,983	$5,289	$2,314	$1,983	$1,653	$2,479	$26,452	$113,418
2017	$11,502	$2,043	$5,448	$2,383	$2,043	$1,702	$2,554	$27,675	$118,730
2018	$12,307	$2,104	$5,611	$2,455	$2,104	$1,754	$2,630	$28,965	$124,335
2019	$13,169	$2,167	$5,780	$2,529	$2,167	$1,806	$2,709	$30,327	$130,250
2020	$14,090	$2,232	$5,953	$2,604	$2,232	$1,860	$2,790	$31,763	$136,497
2021	$15,077	$2,299	$6,132	$2,683	$2,299	$1,916	$2,874	$33,280	$143,094

LIVING AT HOME

Year Start School	Tuition	Books & Supplies	Accommo- dation	Food	Entertain- ment	Transport	Personal Care	Total	Four-Year Total
1999	$3,403	$1,200	$-	$-	$1,200	$500	$1,500	$7,803	$33,517
2000	$3,641	$1,236	$-	$-	$1,236	$515	$1,545	$8,173	$35,127
2001	$3,896	$1,273	$-	$-	$1,273	$530	$1,591	$8,564	$36,827
2002	$4,169	$1,311	$-	$-	$1,311	$546	$1,639	$8,977	$38,624
2003	$4,461	$1,351	$-	$-	$1,351	$563	$1,688	$9,413	$40,523
2004	$4,773	$1,391	$-	$-	$1,391	$580	$1,739	$9,874	$42,531
2005	$5,107	$1,433	$-	$-	$1,433	$597	$1,791	$10,361	$44,655
2006	$5,464	$1,476	$-	$-	$1,476	$615	$1,845	$10,876	$46,901
2007	$5,847	$1,520	$-	$-	$1,520	$633	$1,900	$11,421	$49,279
2008	$6,256	$1,566	$-	$-	$1,566	$652	$1,957	$11,997	$51,796
2009	$6,694	$1,613	$-	$-	$1,613	$672	$2,016	$12,607	$54,461
2010	$7,163	$1,661	$-	$-	$1,661	$692	$2,076	$13,253	$57,283
2011	$7,664	$1,711	$-	$-	$1,711	$713	$2,139	$13,938	$60,274
2012	$8,201	$1,762	$-	$-	$1,762	$734	$2,203	$14,662	$63,443
2013	$8,775	$1,815	$-	$-	$1,815	$756	$2,269	$15,430	$66,803
2014	$9,389	$1,870	$-	$-	$1,870	$779	$2,337	$16,244	$70,366
2015	$10,046	$1,926	$-	$-	$1,926	$802	$2,407	$17,107	$74,144
2016	$10,749	$1,983	$-	$-	$1,983	$826	$2,479	$18,022	$78,152
2017	$11,502	$2,043	$-	$-	$2,043	$851	$2,554	$18,993	$82,406
2018	$12,307	$2,104	$-	$-	$2,104	$877	$2,630	$20,022	$86,921
2019	$13,169	$2,167	$-	$-	$2,167	$903	$2,709	$21,115	$91,714
2020	$14,090	$2,232	$-	$-	$2,232	$930	$2,790	$22,276	$96,805
2021	$15,077	$2,299	$-	$-	$2,299	$958	$2,874	$23,508	$102,211

Estimate of Education Costs - Tuition Inflation At 9 Percent

Assumed inflation for tuition costs   9.00%
Assumed inflation for other costs   3.00%

LIVING AWAY FROM HOME

Year Start School	Tuition	Books & Supplies	Accommo- dation	Food	Entertain- ment	Transport	Personal Care	Total	Four-Year Total
1999	$3,403	$1,200	$3,200	$1,400	$1,200	$1,000	$1,500	$12,903	$55,307
2000	$3,709	$1,236	$3,296	$1,442	$1,236	$1,030	$1,545	$13,494	$57,900
2001	$4,043	$1,273	$3,395	$1,485	$1,273	$1,061	$1,591	$14,122	$60,655
2002	$4,407	$1,311	$3,497	$1,530	$1,311	$1,093	$1,639	$14,788	$63,584
2003	$4,804	$1,351	$3,602	$1,576	$1,351	$1,126	$1,688	$15,496	$66,700
2004	$5,236	$1,391	$3,710	$1,623	$1,391	$1,159	$1,739	$16,249	$70,019
2005	$5,707	$1,433	$3,821	$1,672	$1,433	$1,194	$1,791	$17,051	$73,557
2006	$6,221	$1,476	$3,936	$1,722	$1,476	$1,230	$1,845	$17,905	$77,329
2007	$6,781	$1,520	$4,054	$1,773	$1,520	$1,267	$1,900	$18,815	$81,356
2008	$7,391	$1,566	$4,175	$1,827	$1,566	$1,305	$1,957	$19,786	$85,657
2009	$8,056	$1,613	$4,301	$1,881	$1,613	$1,344	$2,016	$20,823	$90,255
2010	$8,781	$1,661	$4,430	$1,938	$1,661	$1,384	$2,076	$21,931	$95,173
2011	$9,571	$1,711	$4,562	$1,996	$1,711	$1,426	$2,139	$23,116	$100,438
2012	$10,433	$1,762	$4,699	$2,056	$1,762	$1,469	$2,203	$24,384	$106,077
2013	$11,372	$1,815	$4,840	$2,118	$1,815	$1,513	$2,269	$25,741	$112,122
2014	$12,395	$1,870	$4,985	$2,181	$1,870	$1,558	$2,337	$27,196	$118,606
2015	$13,511	$1,926	$5,135	$2,247	$1,926	$1,605	$2,407	$28,756	$125,566
2016	$14,727	$1,983	$5,289	$2,314	$1,983	$1,653	$2,479	$30,429	$133,040
2017	$16,052	$2,043	$5,448	$2,383	$2,043	$1,702	$2,554	$32,225	$141,072
2018	$17,497	$2,104	$5,611	$2,455	$2,104	$1,754	$2,630	$34,155	$149,709
2019	$19,072	$2,167	$5,780	$2,529	$2,167	$1,806	$2,709	$36,230	$159,001
2020	$20,788	$2,232	$5,953	$2,604	$2,232	$1,860	$2,790	$38,461	$169,004
2021	$22,659	$2,299	$6,132	$2,683	$2,299	$1,916	$2,874	$40,862	$179,778

LIVING AT HOME

Year Start School	Tuition	Books & Supplies	Accommo-dation	Food	Entertain-ment	Transport	Personal Care	Total	Four-Year Total
1999	$3,403	$1,200	$-	$-	$1,200	$500	$1,500	$7,803	$33,970
2000	$3,709	$1,236	$-	$-	$1,236	$515	$1,545	$8,241	$35,923
2001	$4,043	$1,273	$-	$-	$1,273	$530	$1,591	$8,711	$38,019
2002	$4,407	$1,311	$-	$-	$1,311	$546	$1,639	$9,215	$40,269
2003	$4,804	$1,351	$-	$-	$1,351	$563	$1,688	$9,756	$42,686
2004	$5,236	$1,391	$-	$-	$1,391	$580	$1,739	$10,337	$45,284
2005	$5,707	$1,433	$-	$-	$1,433	$597	$1,791	$10,961	$48,080
2006	$6,221	$1,476	$-	$-	$1,476	$615	$1,845	$11,632	$51,088
2007	$6,781	$1,520	$-	$-	$1,520	$633	$1,900	$12,354	$54,328
2008	$7,391	$1,566	$-	$-	$1,566	$652	$1,957	$13,132	$57,818
2009	$8,056	$1,613	$-	$-	$1,613	$672	$2,016	$13,969	$61,581
2010	$8,781	$1,661	$-	$-	$1,661	$692	$2,076	$14,872	$65,638
2011	$9,571	$1,711	$-	$-	$1,711	$713	$2,139	$15,845	$70,017
2012	$10,433	$1,762	$-	$-	$1,762	$734	$2,203	$16,894	$74,744
2013	$11,372	$1,815	$-	$-	$1,815	$756	$2,269	$18,027	$79,849
2014	$12,395	$1,870	$-	$-	$1,870	$779	$2,337	$19,250	$85,365
2015	$13,511	$1,926	$-	$-	$1,926	$802	$2,407	$20,572	$91,327
2016	$14,727	$1,983	$-	$-	$1,983	$826	$2,479	$21,999	$97,774
2017	$16,052	$2,043	$-	$-	$2,043	$851	$2,554	$23,543	$104,748
2018	$17,497	$2,104	$-	$-	$2,104	$877	$2,630	$25,212	$112,295
2019	$19,072	$2,167	$-	$-	$2,167	$903	$2,709	$27,019	$120,465
2020	$20,788	$2,232	$-	$-	$2,232	$930	$2,790	$28,974	$129,312
2021	$22,659	$2,299	$-	$-	$2,299	$958	$2,874	$31,090	$138,895

Glossary

One thing is for sure: Learning new rules and strategies in saving for education can be like learning a new language. For your benefit, I've listed here the most important terms you'll find in this book, and their definitions.

Accumulated Income Payment (AIP) This is a payment made to the subscriber out of an RESP's investment earnings, including earnings on the CESG. AIPs are taxable in the hands of the subscriber, and are subject to a 20 percent penalty to boot.

Asset Allocation This is the process of determining which of the three categories of investments you will allocate your investments to. The categories are equity investments, fixed-income investments, and cash. Proper asset allocation will have a greater impact on your investment returns than the selection of individual securities.

Assisted Contributions Contributions made to an RESP after 1997 in respect of which a CESG has been or will be paid.

Beneficiary An individual named by the subscriber of an RESP who will receive Educational Assistance Payments if the individual qualifies for these payments under the terms of the plan.

Canada Education Savings Grant (CESG) A grant paid by Human Resources Development Canada to the RESP trustee for deposit in the RESP account on behalf of the beneficiary. The grant is equal to 20 percent of any contributions made by the subscriber to an RESP, to a maximum of $400 for each year that an eligible child is age 17 or under in the year.

Canada Millennium Scholarship Foundation The 1998 federal budget established a foundation of $2.5 billion with the mandate of paying scholarships to students from low- and middle-income families with a financial need. Beginning in the year 2000, scholarships averaging $3,000 per student per year, to a maximum of $15,000 per student over four years will be handed out to approximately 100,000 students.

Canada Student Loans Program (CSLP) A program under which all loans made by the federal government to students are administered. Ottawa lent $1.62 billion to 350,000 students in 1997–98. The loans are available for both full- and part-time study, but certain criteria must be met to be eligible. More information is available from your child's high school guidance department, university or college financial assistance offices, or through Human Resources Development Canada.

CESG Contribution Room Beginning with 1998, each child who is age 17 or under in the year and who is resident in Canada accumulates "contribution room" at a rate of $2,000 per year. The contribution room accumulates whether or not the child is currently an RESP beneficiary, and any unused contribution room is carried forward. Assisted contributions to an RESP can be made provided there is contribution room available to the beneficiary.

Contributor *See* Subscriber.

Cooperative Study Program A program of study at the postsecondary level that provides work terms for students in the program. The work terms fall between semesters of study at school and can provide valuable work experience that may assist the student in finding work after graduation. Work terms also provide an income to help pay for school.

Educational Assistance Payment (EAP) Any amount paid or payable under an RESP to or for an individual (called the beneficiary) to assist with the individual's education at the postsecondary school level. These amounts do not include refunds of contributions made to the subscriber of the plan. Rather, EAPs are always made out of the accumulated income in the plan, and are taxable to the beneficiary in the year received.

Education Savings Plan A contract entered into at any time between an individual (referred to as a "subscriber") and a person or organization (referred to as a "promoter") under which the promoter agrees to pay or cause to be paid educational assistance payments to or for one or more beneficiaries.

Education Tax Credits *See* Tax Credits.

Equity Investments An investment that provides ownership in an asset that is intended to appreciate in value over time. Stocks, mutual funds that invest in stocks, and real estate are examples of equity investments.

Family Plan Technically called a "multi-beneficiary" plan under the *Income Tax Act*, this is a type of RESP under which one or more beneficiaries can be named. All beneficiaries must be connected to the subscriber by blood or adoption. Further, all beneficiaries must be under age 21 at the time they are named as beneficiaries.

Fixed-Income Investments A marketable security that is intended to provide a steady stream of income, but that has some potential to appreciate in value. Corporate or government bonds and mortgage-backed securities are examples of fixed-income investments.

Foreign Content That portion of an investment account or portfolio that consists of foreign securities, mutual funds that invest in foreign securities, or mutual funds designed to mirror the performance of foreign stock markets or indices. While foreign content restrictions are placed on RRSPs (maximum 20 percent of book value), there are no such restrictions for RESPs. Foreign content will generally help to boost investment returns since foreign markets often outperform the Canadian market.

Group Plan This is a type of RESP that is operated on a pooling principle where the beneficiary named under a contract by a subscriber will receive Educational Assistance Payments when enrolled in a qualifying program, but if the beneficiary fails to qualify for payment, the earnings are distributed among other beneficiaries of the same age who do qualify. These plans are offered by scholarship trust organizations. Group plans can be split into two sub-types: individual plans and family plans.

Individual Plan A type of RESP, the terms of which allow just one beneficiary at any given time. There is no requirement for the beneficiary to be related to the subscriber, and the subscriber can even name himself or his spouse as a beneficiary. Nor is there a requirement that the beneficiary be under any particular age.

Informal Trust *See* In-trust Account.

In-trust Account An investment account opened by an adult for the benefit of a child. The adult will contribute assets (usually cash) to the account. The name of an adult (not necessarily the contributor) will appear on the account with the child's name. The adult whose name appears on the account is the trustee of the account. The purpose of an in-trust account is to have the child pay any tax on capital gains generated in the account. Interest, dividends, or other income earned in the account will be taxed in the hands of the contributor. To ensure capital gains will be taxed in the child's hands, the contributor to the account should not also be the trustee, and the assets in the account must be used exclusively for the child's benefit. Provincial trust law may govern these accounts.

Pooled Plan *See* Group Plan.

Postsecondary Educational Institution Such an institution can be any of the following:

a) A university, college, or other educational institution in Canada that has been designated for purposes of the *Canada Student Loans Act* or the *Canada Student Financial Assistance Act,* or is recognized for purposes of the *Québec Student Loans and Scholarships Act.*

b) An educational institution in Canada certified by the Minister of Human Resources Development to provide courses, other than courses designed for university credit, that give a person occupational skills or improve a person's occupational skills.

c) A university, college or other educational institution outside Canada that provides courses at a postsecondary school level, provided the beneficiary is enrolled in a course that runs at least 13 consecutive weeks.

Promoter The Promoter can be any person or organization offering a Registered Education Savings Plan to the public.

Refund of Contributions A payment to a subscriber that represents a refund of original contributions to the RESP. These can be refunded to the subscriber free of tax. If the terms of the plan permit, these payments can be made to the subscriber at any time.

Registered Education Savings Plan (RESP) A contract between a subscriber and an RESP promoter under which the subscriber makes contributions on behalf of a beneficiary, and the promoter agrees to make Educational Assistance Payments to the beneficiary. The RESP is simply an education savings plan that is registered with Revenue Canada under the *Income Tax Act*.

Registered Retirement Savings Plan (RRSP) A plan registered with Revenue Canada for the purpose of saving for retirement. Assets in the plan grow on a tax-deferred basis. Contributions to an RRSP are deductible for tax purposes, and are subject to certain maximums based on "earned income." Up to $50,000 of RESP assets can be transferred to an RRSP in situations where the beneficiary of the RESP does not pursue an education, and where the subscriber to the RESP has sufficient RRSP contribution room, and certain other conditions are met.

Scholarship Trust *See* Group Plan.

Self-directed RESP This is a type of RESP that generally provides the maximum flexibility in deciding what investments to hold, the timing of payments out of the plan, and the naming of beneficiaries. These plans are available through brokerage and financial planning firms, banks, trust companies, credit unions, and mutual fund companies. The counterpart to a self-directed plan is a group plan. Self-directed plans can be split into two sub-types: individual and family plans.

Subscriber Sometimes referred to as the contributor to an RESP, this is a person who enters into an RESP contract with the promoter. The subscriber is either entitled or required (depending on the contract) to contribute to the RESP on behalf of an individual named under the plan as the beneficiary. If the plan permits, spouses can be joint subscribers. The subscriber must be an individual. A corporation, trust, church, or charity cannot be a subscriber.

Tax Credits Each student is entitled to a tax credit for tuition paid in the year. The combined federal and provincial value of the tuition credit is approximately 26 percent of the tuition paid. In addition, students are entitled to an education tax credit worth approximately 26 percent of a certain amount. This amount is $200 for each month of full-time enrollment in a qualifying program, or $60 for each month of part-time enrollment. Up to $5,000 of tuition and education amounts can be transferred to parents, grandparents, or a spouse if they are not needed by the student to reduce taxes to nil, or can be carried forward for use in the future. Finally, students may be entitled to a credit for interest paid on student loans administered under the Canada Student Loans Program or equivalent provincial program. This interest tax credit will save a student taxes of approximately 26 percent of all interest paid on these student loans in the year, and can be carried forward to be used in any of the subsequent five years if not needed to reduce taxes to nil in the year the interest was paid.

Trustee The *Income Tax Act* requires RESP funds to be held by a corporation licensed to be a trustee. The trustee is engaged by the promoter and can be the promoter itself. The CESG will be provided directly to the plan trustee for deposit into the RESP account.

Tuition Tax Credits *See* Tax Credits.

Unassisted Contributions Contributions made to an RESP in respect of which no CESG has been or will be paid. These include pre-1998 contributions, or contributions made over and above the CESG contribution room available to the child.

We make financial advisors look good. Very good.

Tim Cestnick is not only the author of this book, he is the president of our firm, The WaterStreet Group Inc. We are Canada's leading tax resource to financial advisors from coast to coast. We provide tax education and consulting, and we make advisors look good — very good, in fact. You see, when clients turn to a financial advisor for tax or estate planning help, advisors turn to us.

So let us act on your behalf — no matter where across this country you happen to be. After all, no one understands tax and estate planning issues like we do. And no one is better at creative solutions than we are.

Client seminars	Personal and corporate tax planning
Advisor education and training	Corporate reorganizations
Email tax information service	Individual Pension Plans
Newsletters	Estate planning
Professional writing	Revenue Canada representation

The WaterStreet Group Inc.
420 North Service Road East, Suite 200
Oakville, ON   L6H 5R2
Phone: (416) 410-4410   Fax: (416) 410-4411   Web: www.waterstreet.ca